☆

JOE FRANKLIN'S

JOE FRANKLIN'S MEMORY LANE COOKBOOK

BY
JOE FRANKLIN
WITH
FLORENCE STEVENSON

LION BOOKS
NEW YORK

To my viewers and listeners, this book is affectionately dedicated.

This is a Lion Book
Published by Sayre Publishing, Inc.

Published in the United States by Sayre Publishing, Inc.
111 East 39 St., New York, N.Y. 10016

Library of Congress Cataloging in Publication Data

Franklin, Joe.
Lee Franklin's memory lane cookbook.

1. Cookery. 2. Actors—United States.
I. Stevenson, Florence. II. Title. III. Title:
Memory lane cookbook.

TX715.F836 641.5 70-112375
ISBN 0-87460-242-4

Preface

After much persuasion from people who tune in to my *Memory Lane* TV show as well as my radio program on WOR, I have decided to write the *Memory Lane Cookbook*—a collection of memories and recipes gleaned from my association with the stars of yesteryear or with the people who knew these stars in the days when movies were movies.

Viewers of my *Memory Lane* show know that I have dedicated my present to my past. Nostalgia is my business and, from the letters I receive, I'd guess that many of you are also fond of remembering when. *When* was a great time, wasn't it? When the world was a little younger, a little more naïve, a little more magical. I've been gathering bits and pieces of those days for years. Why am I putting them together in a cookbook? Because I've had so many letters from other memory collectors, asking me about the stars—what they ate, what they wore, where they lived.

I've done a lot of talking to a lot of people, on and off the mike and screen. Some of the greats, like Al Jolson, Eddie Cantor, Rudy Vallee, Paul Whiteman, and Ricardo Cortez, I knew and know very well; my stories about others have come to me from their friends, their colleagues, their relatives.

As for the recipes, I'm playing it safe. Some of them I begged, borrowed, or stole directly from the dining table. For others, I've had to rely on the memories of friends who dined with the stars. So, many of the recipes I'm including in this book are approximations, rather than the real thing. I'll confess I've eaten the entire table of contents—and every recipe in this book has been further tested by my wife Lois and my son Bradley.

Joe Franklin

Three of Joe Franklin's all-time greats: Rudy Vallee, top left: Ricardo Cortez, top right; and getting an earful, none other than Eddie Cantor

☆

CONTENTS

JOE FRANKLIN'S MEMORY LANE COOKBOOK

Robert Montgomery and Janet Gaynor as the stars of *Three Loves Has Nancy*

The Marquise de la Falaise. She was known to fans as Constance Bennett.

From Dolores Del Rio to Robert Montgomery, the stars loved to entertain in their natural habitat: Hollywood. We'll sample Escargots a la Bennett at Constance Bennett's Beverly Hills hacienda, and drop in to share Carrots Petruchka with that connoisseur vegetarian, George Arliss.

☆

CHAPTER 1 HOLLYWOOD AT HOME

☆

Come with me down Memory Lane—and let's wend our way to Hollywood in the early 1930's, when some of the old stars were still shining and some fabulous new names were lighting up the sky. I'm talking about Mary Pickford, Doug Fairbanks, Connie Bennett, Miriam Hopkins—you'll see.

These people came from all over the world to act in movies, and a single picture often took longer than you might imagine. Janet Gaynor, for instance, spent six months making her first hit—*Sunrise.* She finished it around noon one day, went to wardrobe, turned in her blond wig, had lunch in the studio commissary, and then reported for work on the *Seventh Heaven* set. (Just for the record, *Sunrise* was released after *Seventh Heaven,* making it her second first hit. Got it?) Anyhow, such stints made it imperative to settle down someplace in the mythical region of Hollywood—I call it "mythical" because Hollywood in movie parlance is an all-embracing term and, like the fabled L.A. city limits, it covers a lot of territory. In this chapter, you'll find that Hollywood can mean Beverly Hills, Laurel Canyon, Santa Monica, Malibu, Culver City, or Hollywood.

In those days, before the population explosion increased property values on the West Coast, you could buy a house almost more cheaply than you could rent one. Certainly, it was a better investment than holing up in one of the local hotels which, if first class, was more costly than most similar accommodations across the nation. A lot of canny actors bought homes and later rented or sold them to newcomers—many more settled down and stayed. I'll tell you why—it was a beautiful area, especially in those days when we weren't plagued by ecological troubles. Before Los Angeles smog became legendary, the skies over Memory Lane were a deep Liz Taylor blue; yes, they actually bordered on violet. If you looked in one direction, you'd see snow-capped mountains; in the other, there was the Pacific pounding on white sandy shores. Everywhere there were palm trees, tall and skinny, short and squat, some with dates and others with coconuts. The deep gulches that bordered Sunset Boulevard as it wound toward the sea were thick with towering eucalyptus trees, along with pines and cedars, and sycamores. The same sort of vegetation grew on the hills above Hollywood. There were gardens full of bright calla lilies, roses, nasturtiums, chrysanthemums, dahlias, asters, snowballs, snapdragons, sweet peas—as recently as three years ago, I came upon a whole field of scarlet poinsettias! Oleanders pressed against walls, roofs were hung with white and purple wisteria,

The young Janet Gaynor. They wept buckets for her in *Seventh Heaven*.

Janet Gaynor again. If she had saved those clothes, she'd be in style today.

and with magenta bougainvillea vines. And rambler roses, as often as not, clung to garage walls.

Nearly every backyard had at least one orange tree. The streets were lined with pepper or sycamore trees, and houses were divided by towering cedar hedges. Lawns were velvety green, kept so by constantly whirling sprinklers, a reminder that this demi-paradise had been carved out of a desert. The cliffs overlooking the ocean were heavy with purple and white iceplant, shadowed by wind-stunted pine trees. On empty lots red poppies and yellow mustard flowers bloomed; in the spring, tall blue lupins covered the hillsides.

In that period, there were no freeways—some roads were not even paved. Oilwells reared up in unexpected places. There was, and still is to my knowledge, an active well right in the middle of San Vicente Boulevard, not far from Hollywood proper. In those days, too, Wilshire Boulevard, one of the territory's main thoroughfares, was intersected by a park, complete with a casino, a lake, and pleasure boats with striped awnings. It was known as Westlake Park. Later its name was patriotically changed to MacArthur Park, while progress bisected it with that aforementioned Wilshire Boulevard. Farther out on Wilshire were the La Brea tar pits, a wild, semi-rural stretch of land where in deep, treacherous pits of liquid tar the bones of dinosaurs had been found, later dug up, and placed in the Los Angeles County Museum, a site I shall always remember (the museum, not the pits) because of its acres of rose bushes.

No less attractive than the scenery was the climate of southern California—mild and temperate all year long, pleasantly cool at night, even in the summer. Shall I be tactful and not mention the rains? No, I'll be frank. During the winter season, the rains came and kept on coming, lashing the ocean up over the piers, causing landslides in the mountains and floods in the streets. Too, there were the autumn desert winds blowing gusts of hot air before them, stirring up the dust until the skies turned yellow and, worse yet,

The Bennett sisters, Constance and Joan. Back in those days, they both were blondes.

stirring up the snakes and sending them up out of their holes to slither through the dry grasses. Still, compared with the icy streets of Chicago or New York in winter and with the steaming city summers, southern California was a paradise that almost lived up to what the Chamber of Commerce wrote about it.

Now I've given you an idea about the terrain of Memory Lane, let's pay a few visits. Do you like Spanish architecture? We're going to see a lot of it, because that's what they used to build—great big white, yellow, pink, and green stucco homes topped with red tiles—invariably, there was a patio in the rear; sometimes there was a swimming pool and occasionally tennis courts.

Constance Bennett, daughter of the actor Richard Bennett, sister of Joan, was in her heyday in the early thirties—with a mellifluous voice and excellent stage presence, she was a pro to the tips of her crimson fingernails. Blonde and very pretty, she reigned as one of the queens of the films, and in private life, she was a marquise—married to the Marquis de la Falaise. The happy couple settled down (briefly) in a huge hacienda in Beverly Hills. If you had been invited to dine with Connie, you might have been rather surprised by her decor, which she matched to her title rather than to her Spanish-influenced house; it was French, running to cream walls, chairs upholstered in white satin, and windows hung with vivid floral drapes. A length of Chinese embroidery stretched along the wall over her walnut buffet, and in the center of the room, a crystal chandelier shone over her table. However, when Connie gave one of her famed parties, she generally brought out small individual tables for selected groups of guests. As for her cuisine, it was spectacular. Rudy Vallee, who often dined with Connie and the Marquis, can still remember such *pieces de resistances* as the following:

ONION SOUP

3 large onions
4 tbsp. butter
2 quarts beef bouillon
(use either cubes or instant mix)
salt and pepper
6 slices dry French bread
Roquefort cheese

Peel onions and slice very thin. Melt butter in saucepan and sauté onions until golden brown. Gradually stir in bouillon, season with salt and pepper. Cover and simmer gently for 20 minutes.

Rub French bread with Roquefort cheese. Add to soup just before serving. (Serves 6–8)

Not everybody in Hollywood had such an educated palate as Connie did, but for those who liked a touch of the exotic, this dish was just what the doctor (or should I say gardener) ordered:

*ESCARGOTS A LA BENNETT**

4 dozen snails
¾ lb. butter
2 tsp. chopped onion
2 tsp. finely chopped parsley
dash of oregano
2 cloves garlic, crushed
1 tsp. salt
¼ tsp. pepper
⅓ cup breadcrumbs

In mixing bowl put butter, onion, parsley, oregano, garlic, salt, and pepper. Mix thoroughly.

In the bottom of each snail shell put a little bit of the above mixture. Add snail. Fill shell with mixture. Arrange shells, bottoms down, on baking dish. Sprinkle with crumbs. Bake in hot oven (400°) for 8 minutes. Serve hot. (Serves 6–8)

* *Note: Buy canned snails and shells, which come separately.*

Edmund Lowe, puttees and all, turned on the charm in *What Price Glory?*

Another couple who inhabited a Spanish-style house was Edmund Lowe, handsome star of *What Price Glory* and *The Cockeyed World,* and his glamorous wife, Lilyan Tashman. Miss Tashman was Hollywood's best-dressed woman—she was equally well known for her well-furnished houses. I believe it was Lilyan who had the first all-white room in town—even her piano was white, but as far as I am concerned, the topper was the two chairs she had upholstered in ermine!

When you dined with Ed and Lil, you sat in a small dark room that opened onto a simply magnificent patio full of flowers and shrubs. In the dining room, a real Italian renaissance table rested on a rough stone floor, made to simulate castle conditions, I guess. No two of the twelve chairs arranged round that table matched; all were antiques, and varied from a monk's bench to a brocaded side-chair. I know that no one will mind if I let you have Lilyan's recipe for spaghetti, which as it happens is not Italian—it was dreamed up by a Hungarian cook her mother knew.

Lowe was one of the beautiful people.

LILYAN'S SPAGHETTI

1 lb. ground round steak
½ lb. ground pork
2 green peppers, chopped
2 medium-sized onions, chopped
1 clove garlic, minced
1 package dried mushrooms
(softened in water)
½ lb. fresh mushrooms, sliced
¼ lb. butter
salt and pepper, to taste
½ lb. American cheese
½ lb. Cheddar cheese
2 cans tomato sauce
2 packages No. 3 spaghetti

In a saucepan, combine ground round and pork, and brown slightly in butter. Put green peppers, onions, garlic, mushrooms, and butter in a Dutch oven and sauté in butter until onions are transparent and mushrooms soft. Add meat and salt and pepper to taste. Mix thoroughly. Remove from flame.

Boil spaghetti according to directions on package.

Add spaghetti to mixture in Dutch oven. Add chunks of Cheddar cheese and tomato sauce. Mix thoroughly. Top with slices of American cheese. Cover. Put in moderate oven (350°). When top cheese is thoroughly melted—about 20 minutes—remove and serve. (Serves 8)

Mrs. Lowe, glamorous Lilyan Tashman

Norma Shearer and her husband Irving Thalberg lived in that part of Hollywood called Malibu Beach—an exclusive suburb by the sea. Miss Shearer was different; she didn't dwell in Spanish splendor—she and her husband chose a French provincial home which fronted the shore. It had the added attraction of a seaside swimming pool in case the tide was too rough or cold. I bet all of you would really dig her dining room, done in white and green with Louis XVI furniture, but simple, very simple—no carved curlicues here. It was *très élégant*—Franklin's fractured French for swell! As for the food—this side of heaven, and beautifully served. No, it was not necessarily French. Bert Gould, the writer, cribbed these two dishes for me.

SHEER SALMON

5 lbs. salmon
salt and pepper
4 tbsp. butter, melted
4 strips of bacon
1 cup canned tomatoes
½ cup Marsala

Place fish in shallow greased baking dish. Sprinkle with salt and pepper and pour on melted butter. Top with bacon. Add tomato and wine. Cover and bake in moderate oven (350°) for 35 minutes. Uncover, remove bacon. Bake 5 minutes more, or until brown. (Serves 8)

Along with that salmon, how's about some Seaside Salad?

Norma Shearer, one of America's best-loved heroines of the silver screen

SEASIDE SALAD

¼ lb. marshmallows
1 package lemon gelatin
1 package lime gelatin
2 cups hot water
1 No. 2 can crushed pineapple
1 cup Thompson seedless grapes
1 3-oz. package cream cheese, crumbled
½ pint heavy cream, whipped

Melt marshmallows over hot water in top of double boiler. Dissolve gelatin in hot water. Stir some of the gelatin mixture into marshmallows. Blend. Add to remaining gelatin. Stir until marshmallows are dissolved. Cool until slightly thickened. Fold in pineapple, grapes, cheese, and cream. Pour into 8 x 8 x 2-inch mold. Chill until firm. Serve on lettuce with mayonnaise. (Serves 12)

Cheerful for Alexander Kirkland, tearful for Ralph Morgan, Norma Shearer starred in *Romeo and Juliet,* produced by her husband, Irving Thalberg.

In those days, my friend Bob Montgomery was one of filmdom's most handsome young matinee idols. He and his wife lived in a —you guessed it—Spanish house, a large one built around a huge patio graced by an immense pepper tree, which they adored. Some other furnishings of that patio were a goldfish pond, roses, palm trees, and a great mass of bougainvillea over the roof. I could talk on and on about their dining room; it had scenic wallpaper and one of those chandeliers made to look like an old gaslight. Actually, the Montgomerys didn't spend too much time dining indoors; they were crazy about outdoor living, and if they didn't cook their food over a charcoal stove, they had it served outside. As for what they ate, Bob believed in going California all the way, which means steak and salad.

Montgomery ward: Bob in *The Big House* with Chester Morris and Wallace Beery; tops with William Powell and Joan Crawford; with Madge Evans.

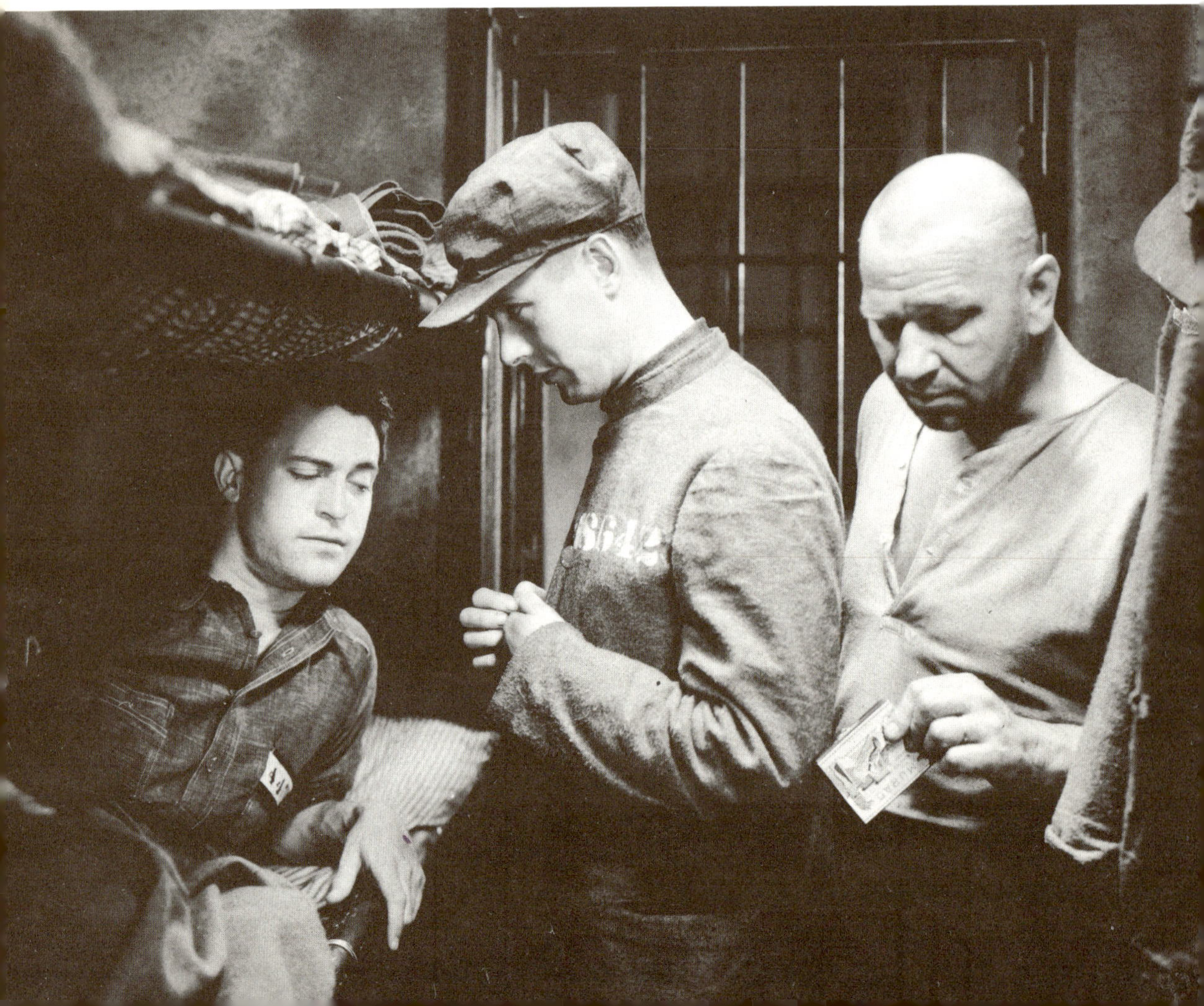

STEAK MONTGOMERY

steak (you name the type)
salt and pepper
garlic clove (or garlic powder)
French dressing

About ½ hour before dining, take the steak from the refrigerator, trim off surplus fat, and add salt and pepper liberally on both sides. With a knife, cut around the edges and insert small slivers of garlic; also insert garlic along the bone if there happens to be one. Then put in shallow pan and soak in French dressing to cover. Broil to suit your taste. (Note: If using powdered garlic, rub on steak with other seasonings.)

SALAD AMIGOS

1 head Romaine or iceberg lettuce
4 tomatoes
¼ cup olive oil
⅓ cup vinegar
salt and pepper
oregano
Roquefort cheese

Break lettuce in pieces. Slice tomatoes. Mix with lettuce. Mix together oil, vinegar, and seasonings, to taste. Add as much cheese as you like. Blend with dressing and pour on salad. Toss. Chill. (Serves 4)

Marie Dressler. Boy, what a lot of memories her name conjures up. She was big box-office, bigger than any of the so-called glamour girls. Can you remember her and Polly Moran knocking their way through all those wild comedies? Can you recall Marie with Wallace Beery in *Min and Bill?* Marie with Greta Garbo in *Anna Christie*—that was the picture in which Garbo spoke, but Marie spoke, too, and darn near stole the whole thing. And in case you think she was always rough and rowdy, let me remind you that she also was quite the grande dame in *Dinner at Eight.* However, she wasn't really prententious, except when she served her own dinners. Maybe you didn't know it, but Marie Dressler was a good cook and when I say good, I mean superlative. She possessed one of the finest collections of recipes in the world, and she

They were hilarious, if not glamorous: Polly Moran and Marie Dressler

Marie Dressler in unaccustomed splendor for *Let Us Be Gay,* with Norma Shearer. Wallace Beery drove his minibus cross-country to Hollywood.

served some of the best dinners in her own little dining room, sitting at the head of her table and dishing out her specialties on immense silver platters. You want to know what she was famous for: her waffle-and-sausage breakfasts. And if you'd like to share one, I have her recipe—yes, her very own! You'll have to furnish the silver platters.

WAFFLES MARIE

2 cups sifted flour
2 tsp. baking powder
⅔ tsp. salt
2 eggs
1¼ cups milk
6 tbsp. melted butter

Sift dry ingredients and mix to a light batter with beaten egg yolks, milk, and melted butter. Beat egg whites until stiff and fold into batter. Bake in a preheated waffle iron for 3 minutes. Serve with butter and syrup. (Serves 2)

Simple, yes—but here are a few variations on the theme!

1. Stir 1 cup grated American cheese into batter.
2. Remove 3 tbsp. flour from the recipe and substitute cocoa.
3. Stir 1½ cups sliced bananas into the batter before folding in the egg.
4. Use 1 tsp. lemon or anise or brandy extract in batter for extra flavor.

As for the sausages, you can suit yourself. I prefer them small and Viennese. The sausages, I mean. J. F.

Miriam Hopkins has always been onc of my favorite actresses. I remember her as the giddy young thing in *The Smiling Lieutenant,* which starred Maurice Chevalier! I saw that at the museum. I also saw her in *These Three,* that moving adaption of Lillian Hellman's *The Children's Hour.* More recently, I was amazed by the versatility of her performance in *Look Homeward, Angel.* But let's stick to older memories. When Miriam bounced into Hollywood, she was petite, blonde, and her tongue was sugar-coated with a soft Georgia-peach accent. Remember what I said about renting? Miriam moved into Garbo's recently

Unlike many an early starlet, Miriam Hopkins really did become a star.

Maurice Chevalier walzes Jeannette MacDonald in *One Hour with You.*

Chevalier again—this time using a touch of Gallic charm on Frances Dee

vacated villa out Benedict Canyon way. It was a Spanish house surrounded with a high I-want-to-be-alone hedge on one side, and several of its large windows faced the distant sea. Miriam loved the ocean view and ignored the hedge—she didn't want to be alone and she wasn't: her gatherings in Garbo's small infromal dining room soon became famous, especially since many of her specialties were southern, traditional, and inherited. Dig that crazy Pecan Pie!

PECAN PIE

9-inch pie shell (packaged mix)
⅓ cup butter
½ cup light brown sugar
½ cup light corn syrup
3 eggs, well beaten
1¼ cups broken pecans
¼ tsp. salt
¾ tsp. vanilla

Prepare pie shell according to directions on package of mix. Bake in moderate oven (350°); when partially done, remove from heat.

Cream butter, add sugar, continue creaming, while adding liquids. Blend thoroughly, then beat in eggs with nuts, salt, and vanilla. Turn into partially baked pie shell and return to moderate oven (350°) for 20 minutes, or until no filling adheres to the tip of your knife. Serve cold with whipped cream topping. (Serves 6)

We did mention Georgia peaches, didn't we? Have some, southern style:

PEACH MERINGUE

6 canned peach halves
6 sponge cake rounds
2 egg whites
¼ cup powdered sugar
¼ tsp. vanilla

Drain peaches and arrange round side up in a buttered baking pan on rounds of cake.

Meringue: Beat egg whites stiff, gradually adding sugar and vanilla.

Cover peaches with meringue, bake in moderate oven (350°) for 10–15 minutes until delicately browned. (Serves 6)

PEACH SOUFFLÉ

1 cup peach pulp
grated rind of 1 lemon
1 tbsp. lemon juice
½ cup sugar
⅛ tsp. salt
2 egg whites

To make pulp, peel peaches and press through coarse sieve. Add lemon rind and juice, half the sugar, and salt. Beat egg whites until stiff but not dry, beat in the remaining sugar. Fold in pulp, turn into buttered baking dish, set this in a pan of hot water, bake in a moderate oven (375°) for ½ hour or until set. Serve immediately, topped with fresh sliced peaches. (Serves 4)

What about a nice peanut dessert? Another southern favorite:

PEANUT BRITTLE TRIFLE

1 cup heavy cream
¼ lb. peanut brittle, chopped fine
1 cup cooked rice (quick rice will do)
1 cup shredded pineapple
8 marshmallows, chopped
2 tbsp. pineapple juice
powdered sugar to taste
candied cherries

Whip cream until fluffy. Fold in brittle. Add rice, pineapple, and marshmallows. Add pineapple juice and sugar. Put into glass serving dish, add candied cherries, and serve cold. (Serves 4)

It was a great day for the young in heart but portly in figure when Emil Jannings, the great stage and screen idol from Berlin, arrived in Hollywood. This brilliant but hefty actor was to the fat man what Yul Brynner was later to the bald—he made them romantic. After Jannings had appeared in *Greed, The Way of All Flesh,* and *The Blue Angel* nearly everybody loved a fat man. I loved him, too, when I saw a reissue of *The Blue Angel,* in which he ruined himself for the sultry, seductive Marlene Dietrich. But why not—what a way to go! On the screen Jannings was villainous or virtuous by turns, but always fascinating. Would you believe that he received as much fan mail as John Gilbert?

In private life, however, Jannings was the conservative type; he lived very quietly in a large Spanish house in Beverly Hills. Guess what he had in his backyard? Not a swimming pool. No tennis courts. He had a barnyard! His breakfast was always enhanced by a fresh egg—and more often than not, his meals were chicken dinners.

Hero and villain by turns, Emil Jannings faces despair in *The Last Laugh.* In *The Blue Angel,* he faced ruin for the sultry young Marlene Dietrich.

The later Dietrich: *Destry Rides Again* and *Witness for the Prosecution*

FRIED CHICKEN JANNINGS

1 fryer, disjointed
1 egg
¼ cup milk
½ cup seasoned breadcrumbs and flour mixed
¼ lb. butter

Wash chicken. Mix together egg and milk. Dip chicken in mixture, roll in breadcrumbs and flour. Fry in butter in large iron skillet until brown on all sides. Put into buttered baking dish and cover. Bake in moderate oven (350°) for ½ hour. (Serves 4)

HONEY HEN

¼ lb. butter
1 fryer, disjointed, or two large chicken breasts, not deboned
½ cup honey
juice of 1 lemon

Melt butter in a large iron skillet. Add chicken, honey, and lemon juice. Fry until well done. (Serves 2–4)

From Mexico came Lupe Velez, famous as one of Hollywood's freest spirits.

Whenever I think about Lupe Velez, I seem to hear in my mind's ear a rapid-fire, Mexican-accented delivery of words arranged to make you laugh. She had a wonderful sense of humor and, I might add, of timing, too. She could sing a little, act a little, dance a little, but somehow it added up to a lot. Lupe was wild; today's youth would recognize her as a kindred spirit. She did what she wanted when she wanted to do it. Meals at her huge Mexican hacienda could take place at any time, and from what I know about her, the best one was breakfast, which La Lupe prepared herself. She really had a way with eggs.

HUEVOS VELEZ

4 eggs
¼ cup milk
¼ tsp. chili powder
4 slices bacon, crumbled
½ green pepper, minced
½ onion, minced
salt and pepper to taste

Combine eggs with chili powder, bacon, green pepper, and onion. Beat until thoroughly mixed. Add seasoning. Scramble in butter or in Teflon pan. (Serves 2–4)

When I think of Lupe Velez, I am reminded of a kitten, but when I recall Dolores Del Rio, who also came from Mexico, I think of a sleek, sensuous cat. Truly, Miss Del Rio was—and, I might add, still is—one of Mexico's most beautiful exports. Do you know how she came to Hollywood? It had to do with a dinner.

Miss Del Rio, a member of a fine Mexican family, had been destined only for the role of a society hostess. She had married a rich Castilian nobleman and lived with him in a beautiful house in Mexico City. Though she was related to the film star Ramon Novarro, Miss Del Rio had never entertained any movie ambitions until the arrival of four people from filmdom. They were Edwin Carewe, Mary Aiken, Claire Windsor, and Bert Lytell. They had come to town to scout locations for a new picture, and they were combining business with the pleasure of being on their honeymoons. Naturally, Miss Del Rio invited them to dinner. What happened then I shall let her describe. "They came from the country, hot, dusty, tired—and they were an hour late. All of them were so embarrassed that I decided to put them at ease by singing to them."

Dolores's voice and beauty were a combination that could put anybody at ease—and that foursome was no exception. When she finished her little program, Edwin Carewe told Dolores's husband that the lady had definite film potential, and that if she ever came to Hollywood, he would be glad to help her. "My husband and I discussed it—he did not want me to go, but finally

The tempestuous Dolores Del Rio starred in *Bird of Paradise* and *Ramona.*

he consented. He thought I would tire of the life quickly, but . . ."

At that important dinner, Dolores served:

VEGETABLES DEL RIO GRANDE

1 cup raw spinach, chopped
1 green pepper, chopped
1 cup celery, chopped
1 small cucumber, chopped
1 small onion, minced
1 tbsp. raisins
½ tsp. sugar
1 tsp. chili powder
½ tsp. ground cumin powder
¼ tsp. salt
½ cup tomato juice
2 tbsp. dry seasoned breadcrumbs
½ cup grated Cheddar cheese
2 tbsp. butter

Grease a casserole; add vegetables and raisins. In small cup, blend sugar, chili powder, cumin powder, and salt. Mix into vegetables; moisten with tomato juice. Sprinkle crumbs over mixture. Add grated cheese, dot with butter. Preheat oven to 375° and bake 20 minutes. Serve hot from casserole. (Serves 4)

Dolores Del Rio eventually settled down in Hollywood and married Cedric Gibbons, after, of course, divorcing that first, disapproving husband. She became one of Hollywood's most famous hostesses as well as a favorite star.

Equally attractive to the ladies was the aforementioned cousin, Ramon Novarro. Ramon Novarro was something of a mystery man. Everybody speculated about the handsome star, wondering how he spent the millions he made in such spectaculars as *Ben Hur, The Pagan Love Song, Mata Hari,* and *The Son-Daughter.* It was hinted that he meant to retire to a monastery when he was through with Hollywood. Actually, when he was through with Hollywood, he went to France and made pictures there. However, that is another scenario. Novarro's home—all glass and timber—topped a Hollywood hill. His dining room furniture was steel and leather and chromium, but take heart—his meals were Mexican, and those fortunate few who were invited to dine with him said that Hollywood in gaining a movie star had lost a magnificent chef. Want to try some Tamale Pie?

TAMALE PIE

3 long red chili peppers
1½ lbs. chuck
1½ lbs. lean pork
1 medium red onion, diced
¼ tsp. garlic powder
3 8-oz. cans tomato sauce
2 cups water
salt and pepper, to taste
24 ripe olives, pitted (save juice)
¼-oz. bottle stuffed olives (save juice)
24 large, seeded raisins
4 cups water
2 tsp. salt
1 cup butter
2 cups yellow corn meal

Boil red chili peppers, chop in blender, save juice. Cut meat in very small pieces. Add onion and garlic powder, tomato sauce, seasonings, and juices; cook until meat is tender. Add olives and raisins. Heat water to boiling. Add salt and butter. Stir in corn meal slowly. Cook over low heat, stirring constantly until thickened. Line large casserole with corn-meal mixture, leaving portion for top. Add meat with gravy to the corn meal. Top with remaining corn meal. Bake in moderate oven (350°) 1 hour. (Serves 4–6)

Fans swooned over Ramon Novarro. Here, he consoles Jeannette MacDonald.

And here's another Novarro special!

CALDO DE FRIJOLES
Mexican Bean Soup

1 cup pinto beans or red kidney beans
1 quart cold water
salt, to taste
2 green onions (use tops, too), chopped
1 clove garlic
5 sprigs parsley
pulp of 1 green or red hot chili pepper or
1½ tsp. chili powder
1 tsp. oregano
1 cup beef broth

Wash beans. Soak in cold water overnight. Drain, add cold water. Simmer 4–6 hours, adding boiling water as needed. Add salt, onions, garlic, parsley, chili and oregano. Boil until tender. Rub through colander and reheat, adding hot broth until soup is puree consistency. Serve with small rounds of cheese toast. (Serves 4–6)

All this Mexican food makes my mouth water and puts me in the mood for Chili con Carne. Hey, Warner! In case you're wondering who Warner is, I'm thinking about that fabulous star of *Forty-Second Street,* the movie with Ruby Keeler. Remember? Or maybe you saw my friend in *The Prisoner of Shark Island* or in all the other movies he made. Warner Baxter. Warner was the

Ruby Keeler kicked up her heels in Busby Berkeley's *Forty-Second Street.*

Mayor of Malibu, too—and he was a marvelous cook. In fact, I don't know how he kept his weight down; maybe it was all the swimming he did in what his friends called Baxter's back-yard—the Pacific Ocean.

BAXTER'S CHILI CON CARNE

1 lb. dried Mexican pinto beans or red kidney beans
3 pints cold water
1½ tsp. salt
4 tbsp. suet
2 medium onions, sliced
3 cloves garlic, halved
2 tbsp. chili powder
2 tbsp. flour
2 lbs. beef steak, coarsely chopped
3 cups canned tomatoes, liquid reserved
1 cup chopped celery
1 cup black olives, halved
1½ tsp. salt, additional
1 tsp. sugar
1 tsp. dried marjoram
½ tsp. ground cumin seed
canned tortillas

Wash beans, drain. Pour cold water into skillet; add beans to water, add salt. Heat to boiling point over high flame, reduce flame, and cover. Simmer gently 1½ hours, or until beans are soft. Remove from heat. Allow beans to cool in liquid. When cool, measure liquid. If less than 1 cup, add enough cold water to make 1 cup.

Melt suet in a Dutch oven over medium flame; add onions. Sauté 5 minutes, add garlic, sauté 5 more minutes. Remove suet and garlic, stir in chili powder. Flour meat lightly, place in Dutch oven, brown 10 minutes, stirring constantly; cover meat with tomatoes and liquid; add all seasonings, celery and olives. Simmer gently for 30 minutes until meat is tender; add beans and liquid; heat thoroughly. Spoon chili on tortillas and fold. (Serves 10)

Dashing Warner Baxter. He played the lead in *Prisoner of Shark Island.*

I told you we were going to range far and wide in this strictly pot-luck chapter. Now we'll visit that great character actor–star George Arliss. Arliss used to complain humorously that whenever the fan magazines ran out of anything to say about him they fell back on his habit of drinking tea. I can understand that it must have surprised the studio people, though, because George had high tea at four, and nothing prevented him from taking it, not even the fact that cameras were grinding. (Tea can become rather costly that way, old chap.)

Arliss and his wife lived in Hollywood for ten years—from 1928 to 1938. During that time, Arliss appeared as Disraeli, Cardinal Richelieu, and Voltaire—just a few of his scores of unequalled character portrayals. I'd better add *The House of Rothschild,* too—that was one of his best. When he was in town, Arliss lived in a large (yes, it was Spanish-style) house in the Los Feliz Hills. A meal with the Arlisses was meatless; he loved animals and therefore refused to eat them. By the way, he was president of the Anti-Vivisection League, too. His cook had, they say, a way with vegetables. We are including some of the Arliss staples.

Voltaire and Cardinal Richelieu were two of George Arliss's meaty roles.

CARROTS PETRUCHKA

1 pint large carrots
salted water to cover
1 tsp. minced parsley
1 tsp. sugar
½ tsp. paprika
juice of ½ lemon

Peel carrots, dice, and put in water, simmer until tender. Drain and add parsley, sugar, paprika, and lemon juice. Return to fire and cook until hot, shaking the pot so the carrots will not stick. (Serves 4)

HOLLAND CABBAGE

1 small red cabbage
water
1 tbsp. butter, melted
1 tbsp. vinegar
1 tbsp. sugar
salt and pepper

Shred cabbage, cover with water, and let stand for 1 hour. Drain and place in saucepan with melted butter. Add vinegar, sugar, and seasonings. Cover and simmer for ½ hour. (Serves 4)

Greta Garbo, no longer alone, fell for [illegible] *[illegible]el.*

Three immortals, surrounded by mystery: Garbo, Valentino, Barrymore. Greta Garbo wanted to be alone, but she had to eat—and she shared specialties like Swedish Meatballs with a few close, favored friends. In his red-and-black dining room, Rudolph Valentino served Shrimp and Yellow Rice Jambalaya. And don't forget to try one of John Barrymore's recipes—his brandy nightcap called The Sun, for instance.

☆

CHAPTER 2
BY INVITATION ONLY

☆

We are now approaching a very special sector of Memory Lane. The people we will visit lived miles apart but they had one thing in common—fame, enduring and everlasting. Tell me, has anyone ever forgotten Rudolph Valentino, Greta Garbo, or John Barrymore?

These three had something else in common—mystery. No one ever knew the real Valentino, Garbo still remains an enigma, and who can fathom the tragedy of John Barrymore? But we won't talk of tragedies here. Since we are walking up Memory

Lane, we can pick and choose the moments that we spend with our hosts, and as this is a cookbook, they will be festive occasions. We'll start with Rudolph.

Let's look at him the way he was—darkly handsome, sensuous, sinuously graceful. He moved like a dancer; in fact he began his career as a dancer in cabarets and in the theater. He joined a road show in New York; when the show closed Valentino was stranded—flat broke—in San Francisco. Someone told him he ought to try motion pictures. And someone else told him that Al Jolson and his entire company were leaving for Los Angeles in a private train Jolson had chartered. Rudy asked for a berth and Jolson readily agreed to give him the free ride. After a little more good fortune, Rudy got a bit part in a picture and, well—need I go on?

Everybody has heard about Rudy's famed Falcon Lair, his second house in Hollywood. I prefer to talk about his first, which was located in a part of town called Whitely Heights. That's not far from the Hollywood Bowl. Rudy's house hugged the hillside and was more interesting inside than out—there were a living room with black marble floors and cerise draperies at the windows, a red-and-black dining room complete with Chinese red lacquer furnishings upholstered in black satin, a yellow-and-black bedroom. All this black was not because Rudy had a dour disposition; his wife, one Winifred De Wolfe Hudnut, or Natacha Rambova*, as she chose to be known, thought that Rudy ought to have an exotic setting. Fortunately, when it came to the menu,

* *Just a word about Natacha Rambova—she discovered Myrna Loy, and gave that actress her first big break.*

Vilma Banky avoids Valentino's eyes; one glance conquers Agnes Ayres.

Rudy's choice prevailed. Among his other assets, he was quite a gourmet.

CRAB VALENTINO

1 head lettuce
1 heart plus several inner stalks celery, minced
1 lb. crab meat
lemon juice and paprika, to taste
3 tomatoes
3 hard-boiled eggs
2 artichoke bottoms

Shred lettuce and make a bed of it on a platter. Sprinkle minced celery over this. Arrange crab meat on this, having first sprinkled it with lemon juice and paprika. Quarter tomatoes, eggs, and artichoke bottoms and arrange on platter.

In a bowl put:

2 tbsp. chili sauce
2 tbsp. chopped pimento
1 tsp. Worcestershire sauce
1 tsp. salt
1 tsp. powdered sugar
1 tsp. paprika and black pepper, mixed
¼ tsp. English mustard
1 cup mayonnaise

Mix and spread on crab. (Serves 2–4)

Valentino, the legend. They shivered in delight at his sizzling magnetism.

SHRIMP AND YELLOW RICE JAMBALAYA

1 onion, finely chopped
1 clove garlic
1 cup washed uncooked rice
olive oil
1 cup sweet peas
2 pimentos, cut in strips
2 sweet pickled cucumbers, finely sliced
1 green pepper, cut in strips
¼ oz. saffron
2 cups water
1 lb. raw shrimp, peeled and cleaned
few drops yellow food color
salt and pepper, to taste

Brown onion, garlic, and rice in olive oil. Stir until every grain is separate and covered with a film of oil. Add peas, pimentos, cucumbers, and pepper, saffron and water—then add shrimp and yellow food color. When mixture comes to a boil, season with salt and pepper. Stir. Put top on pan and place in hot oven (400°) for 20 minutes. (Serves 4)

Would you like to know a little incidental information about Rudy? He was a well-educated man; he read books in several languages, including Latin, and he was particularly interested in researching the background of the roles he played. He did not want to be a conventional Hollywood pretty-boy—he wanted authenticity and insisted upon it. As an example, take his costuming for *The Son of the Sheik*—here it is, complete with costs:

SON OF THE SHEIK

(Note: This is not a recipe, so don't try it on your stove.)

sapphire ring set in platinum $5,000
antique silver bracelet $150
wristwatch $150
jeweled cigarette lighter $150
jeweled cigarette case $300
turban $25
2 Arabian burnooses $450
2 silk headdresses $70
2 lamb's wool shirts $100
2 embroidered vests $300
sash $20
gold embroidered cloak $500
2 jeweled belts $600
embroidered holster $25

Arabian trousers $175
breeches trimmed with braid $75
2 pairs imported boots $155
slippers $30
antique belt and knife $350
sword $4,000
spurs $50

You suppose that sword was made of solid gold? And as for the ring—since it was black-and-white film, don't you suppose he could have used a fake stone? Oh, well. Mine not to reason why.

Valentino really took his work seriously, and not just in the costume department. At one luncheon, he spoke to the cast and crew of a film he was about to begin. "Remember, we are not making a Valentino picture but *Monsieur Beaucaire* and everybody in the picture is just as important as I am, and I want you all to feel so."

P. G. Wodehouse, an author I admire, served his time in Hollywood and emerged with some hilarious short stories about the industry. One concerned the producer whose servants always turned out to have movie aspirations and were in the habit of reciting Kipling's "Boots" at odd moments. Though Wodehouse was being strictly satirical, the situation is not without its real-life parallels. Take the case of Greta Garbo. Stipulating that the couple she wished to hire must speak Swedish, Miss Garbo contacted them through a Swedish agency and appeared well satisfied with one Gustaf Nord and his wife Sigurd. Actually, neither Gustaf nor his wife had ever been in domestic service. He was the son of a famed Swedish athlete and a graduate of Stockholm's

Royal Dramatic School, where Garbo herself had studied. The couple had come to Hollywood to try for the movies and had taken the position with Garbo because they thought she might be able to help them. However, in the year they stayed with the star, they did not dare broach the subject. Garbo, they learned, was as unapproachable at home as she was on the set and in public.

Romantic roles were made for Garbo. One of her best was Anna Karenina.

I don't believe the Nords ever regretted their imposture, however, for even though they found Garbo rather exacting, they were as fascinated as anyone else by the few personal glimpses she revealed. Life at 1027 Chevy Chase Drive, the address of the great Spanish house the star rented, was as unpredictable as her moods. Though she generally breakfasted in bed, she rose several hours before that to swim in her pool. She had dinner wherever she

Garbo played the captivating Marguerite in *Camille,* with Henry Daniell.

happened to be in the house, or outside in the garden. An insomniac, she often felt hungry in the middle of the night, when she would wake the Nords and insist they talk to her, a whim that made life a little strenuous for them.

Garbo, they discovered, rarely entertained, but when she did, she insisted on serving smorgasbord; that was in the days before she discovered Gayelord Hauser and blackstrap molasses. If you would like to know what it was like to dine with Garbo, I suggest you scan the following:

SMORGASBORD

(This is a typical menu.)

Swedish Rye Bread and Hard Biscuits
Butter

Swedish Caviar

Cold Boiled Tongue
Herring Salad
Swedish Meatballs
Small Boiled Potatoes

Cheese
Pickled Herring

Steamed Spareribs
Mackerel in Aspic
Omelet Soufflé
Anchovy or Herring Temptation

Coffee and Cakes

She retired at the peak of her fame, and fans never found another Garbo.

HERRING TEMPTATION

1 small herring
3–4 raw potatoes
1 small onion
butter
1 cup cream

Clean herring, soak overnight. Remove skin and bones. Cut filets in ½-inch slices. Peel and prepare shoestring potatoes. Peel and mince onion and brown slightly in butter. Grease baking dish and make alternate layers of potatoes, herring, and onion. Be sure that potatoes are on top and bottom of dish. Pour cream over this. Bake 1 hour at 375°. During last 20 minutes of baking cover the dish. If too dry, add more cream. (Serves 4)

HERRING SALAD

2 salt herrings
1½ cups cooked hamburger
1½ cups cooked beets
2 cups cooked potatoes
3 raw apples
1 or 2 medium-sized dill pickles
2 tbsp. sugar
5 tbsp. vinegar
pepper to taste
2 hard-boiled eggs (optional)
3 or 4 boiled beets, parsley (optional)
whipped cream (optional)

Clean and soak herring overnight. Clean, bone, and cut in filets. If too salty, soak more. Dice herring, hamburger, beets, potatoes, apples, and pickles and mix in large bowl. Add sugar, vinegar, pepper. Taste for seasoning purposes. Pack tightly on platter or in mold. Chill in refrigerator for 3 hours. (Serves 4)

Note: The Swedish cook would top the salad with whipped cream tinted red with beet juice (or vegetable coloring), add halved hard-boiled eggs, parsley, and make rosettes from beets.

OMELET SOUFFLÉ

4 tbsp. butter
4 tbsp. flour
2 cups cream
4–5 eggs (separate yolks)
salt and pepper, to taste

Make a Béchamel sauce: heat butter, add flour, stir to golden paste. Add cream gradually. Cook a few moments. Remove from fire, add egg yolks a little at a time. Season. Cool a little before folding in beaten whites of eggs. Pour into buttered floured baking dish. Place in 375° oven and bake until brown. (Serves 4)

EGGS IN MUSTARD SAUCE

6 to 8 hard-boiled eggs, peeled

Mustard Sauce:
3 tbsp. butter
4 tbsp. flour
2½ cups milk
salt and pepper, to taste
prepared mustard, to taste

Heat butter and flour, and stir to golden paste. Add milk gradually, stirring to avoid lumps. Add seasoning and let simmer 8–10 minutes. Halve hard-boiled eggs, cover with sauce, and serve cold. (Serves 4)

EGGS IN TOMATO SAUCE

4–5 hard-boiled eggs, peeled
1 onion
3 tbsp. butter
3 tbsp. tomato sauce
3 tbsp. sauterne
salt, paprika, chopped parsley
breadcrumbs

Slice eggs thin and place in layers on greased baking dish. Peel and mince onion very fine, sauté in butter. Add tomato sauce, wine, and seasonings, simmer 15 minutes. Pour over eggs. Sprinkle with breadcrumbs and bake until golden in 400° oven. (Serves 4)

Gustaf has been quoted as saying that Garbo's very favorite salad was made from vegetables. She ate that with and without smorgasbord.

VEGETABLE SALAD

1 whole medium-sized cauliflower
2 bunches carrots
1 lb. fresh string beans
2 lbs. fresh young peas
(or 2 packages frozen peas)
corn from two cooked ears
2 tsp. lemon juice
salt and pepper to taste
parsley, sliced tomatoes, or radishes
1 cup mayonnaise or French dressing

Squeeze lemon juice over cauliflower. Cook in boiling salted water until done. Scrape and cut carrots in long strips. Cook all vegetables separately. Cover with French dressing or mayonnaise after mixing. (Serves 4)

SWEDISH MEATBALLS

¾ cup dry breadcrumbs
1 onion, minced
2 lbs. chuck (or 1¾ lbs. chuck and ¼ lb. pork), ground
2 eggs
2 cups water for moistening breadcrumbs
2 boiled potatoes, mashed
3 tsp. salt
½ tsp. pepper
¼ lb. butter
Gravy:
3 tbsp. butter
½ cup flour
3–4 cups water
salt and pepper, to taste

Add water gradually to moisten breadcrumbs. Brown onion. Mix meat, eggs, breadcrumbs, potato, onion, and seasonings in large bowl. Melt ¼ lb. butter in frying pan. Shape meat into small balls and brown. When done, remove and add more until mixture is entirely used up.

Make gravy in the same pan. Heat butter and add flour. Stir into golden paste. Add water gradually, stirring to avoid lumps. Season to taste. Pour over meatballs and serve. (Serves 4)

I wish that I could say that I had shared some of Garbo's smorgasbord, but I can't. In fact, I've seen her only twice—at a distance—and each time she did not quite fit the descriptions I had heard about her. The first time was a few years ago. I spotted Miss Garbo in the Beverly Hills Hotel. She was smartly dressed in black, and made no effort to conceal her very lovely features as she walked through the lobby. She hurried up to a tall, distinguished-looking man and flung her arms around him. As loudly as Tallulah Bankhead at her best, she exclaimed, "Dahling!"

My second brief non-encounter took place as I drove along a California highway. Suddenly the car in front of me pulled over to the side of the road to discharge Miss Garbo. I stopped to watch as she ran across the fields, gathering wildflowers. Clutching them, she quickly ran back to the waiting car and disappeared. I haven't run into her since those two brief glimpses in California, although she lives in New York during the months she does not spend at her retreat in Switzerland.

John Barrymore, an Aquarius, was born on February 15, 1882. That date meant a great deal to him, for he believed in astrology and would not start a picture unless his planetary aspects were favorable.

As a young man, Barrymore had a definite talent for drawing. While he was still in his teens, one of his drawings, "The Hangman," was bought by the tycoon Andrew Carnegie for ten dollars. Later, Barrymore landed a job as an illustrator on *The New York Evening Journal*. However, it was inevitable that he would follow his brother Lionel and sister Ethel onto the stage. The Barrymores could trace their acting ancestry back to 1752 and even farther. To John, acting came easily, but, if he was supremely talented, he was never quite happy in his chosen profession. He didn't like actors, and—let's face it—he didn't like himself much, either. In common with many people who seem to have a super-ego, Barrymore really had a super-inferiority complex. Eventually, it destroyed him. But that sad story need not concern us here. We are going to follow him to Hollywood, back in 1925, when he took up permanent residence in that starry citadel.

At that time, Barrymore—with such triumphs as *Hamlet* behind him—was forty-three. He admitted to being forty. He had been married and divorced twice, first from Katherine Harris, a debutante, and then from Michael Strange, a woman who wrote poetry. In Hollywood, he fell in love with the beautiful blonde Dolores Costello, daughter of the matinee idol Maurice Costello and sister of the actress Helene. After a courtship, much of which

Madge Evans offers a cool cheek to John Barrymore in *Dinner at Eight.*

took place while they were filming *The Sea Beast,* a version of *Moby Dick,* John and Dolores were married on November 24, 1928.

The couple moved into what Hollywood wags had already nicknamed "The House that Jack Built," situated on Tower Road, which was on the crest of a spur of Hollywood mountains. From that smogless aerie, you could see the ocean, and on a clear day, if not forever, undoubtedly to Catalina. Jack's house was actually two houses built in the Mexican manner around a huge patio. Each house had windows protected by iron grilles, the roofs were covered with red handmade tiles, winding steps led to a garden full of rare tropical plants, including a tree which had cost $1,800. I understand that it was really intended for a Japanese princess, before Barrymore snagged it from an Osaka nursery. Just so he could get plenty of exercise, he had two swimming pools and a trout pond installed. On the terrace, striped Venetian poles held aloft a huge silken canopy, and that is where Dolores and John usually dined.

Inside, the house was lavishly furnished with art treasures the star had brought from all over the world. In addition to costly Renaissance oils, he also had a huge collection of fine books, many of which were priceless first editions. Naturally there was a bar, or what he called an "English tavern room." In this salon—or should I say saloon—was an authentic frontier bar, which he had purchased in Alaska and had shipped home.

Talking about bars brings me around to the recipe part of this memory. As I mentioned, Barrymore used to pal around with a lot of New York newspapermen in the days before Prohibition made liquor a dirty word. He and his friends visited numerous Broadway taverns and the following drinks were to be found in many of these hostelries. In case some of the ingredients seem strange to you, bear in mind that they were invented well over eighty years ago. Don't try too many at once or you'll end up with an antique hangover.

Lionel Barrymore was a compelling Rasputin. That's sister Ethel at right.

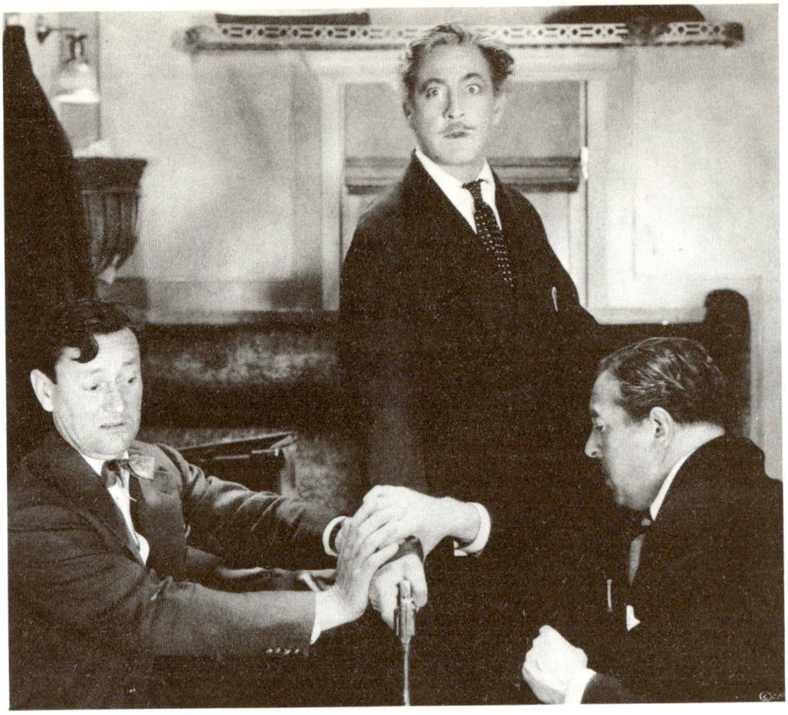

John Barrymore is overcome in *Twentieth Century*. Roscoe Kearns, left.

ORIENTAL BRANDY SOUR

Into a blender squeeze

the juice of ½ lemon and add:
1 tsp. sugar
juice of ½ orange
white of 1 egg
1 shot (1½ oz.) peach brandy

Fill glass with cracked ice,
shake to freezing point, and strain.

ABSINTHE COCKTAIL
(for Absinthe read Pernod)

1 goblet shaved ice and:
2 dashes maraschino
1 dash orange bitters
1 dash anisette
1 shot absinthe

Stir very well, strain into cocktail glass, and serve.

THE ANGELUS

Fill 1 large glass two-thirds full of fine ice with:

1 dash gum
1 dash absinthe
a little vermouth
1 shot gin
2 dashes orange bitters
1 dash curaçao

Stir well and strain.

THE ANTICIPATION
(of what, I wonder?)

1 glass with fine ice, and:

1 dash absinthe
2 dashes gum
¾ oz. sherry wine
¾ oz. vermouth

Freeze well, strain, and serve.

THE BEGINNER

1 goblet with fine ice, and:

2 dashes gum
2 dashes orange bitters
1 dash absinthe
½ shot French vermouth
½ shot Russian kummel

Stir well, strain, and serve.

THE FIRST ONE

1 goblet with fine ice, and:

2 dashes gum
¼ shot crème de menthe
1 shot gin
1 dash orange bitters

Add twist of lemon, stir well, strain, and serve.

THE SUN

Into 1 large thin glass, squeeze juice of ½ orange and ½ lime, add 1 tsp. powdered sugar and dash of mineral water. Add:

1 shot fine brandy
½ shot Jamaica rum
1 dash benedictine
1 dash curaçao
1 dash crème de roses

Mix thoroughly, fill glass with fine ice, stir well; ornament with real snow in the center and write on the snow "The Sun." (And then watch that sun go down.)

THE SENATOR

In 1 glass with shaved ice:

⅙ brandy
⅙ maraschino
⅙ curaçao
⅙ chartreuse
⅙ benedictine
⅙ crème de roses

Shake well, strain into cocktail glass, and serve.

LE FIN DU SIÈCLE

A cocktail shaker with:

the juice of ½ orange
the juice of ¼ lemon
½ tbsp. sugar
1 egg yolk
½ shot brandy
½ shot benedictine
½ shot maraschino
1 dash curaçao
1 dash anisette
1 dash parfait amour
1 dash crème de noyau
3 shots pure cream

Fill shaker with fine ice, shake well; strain into old-fashioned glass; ornament with white of egg that you have beaten up to the form of frozen snow and sweetened with sugar. Serve with a spoon.

Chaplin, Fairbanks, and in the middle, America's sweetheart, Mary Pickford

Hollywood has always been a party town, but never more so than during the twenties and thirties. Douglas Fairbanks and Mary Pickford reigned as host and hostess supreme at their mansion, Pickfair, but Marion Davies was not to be outdone. Try her California Hors d'Oeuvres and Champagne Punch.

☆

CHAPTER 3 PARTY TIME

☆

If I were to talk about Hollywood's party history, I wouldn't have space for anything else. All I can tell you is that Hollywood was and is a party town, and during the late twenties and early thirties, there was something doing every night—the town was really jumpin'!

While there were plenty of glittering hostesses (everybody, and I mean everybody, got into the act), the two that stick in my mind are that little girl with the curls, Mary Pickford, and Marion Davies.

Mary Pickford and her husband, Douglas Fairbanks, Sr., did their entertaining at their hilltop mansion, Pickfair. And it is said that their guest list often read like Burke's Peerage. In her time, America's erstwhile sweetheart welcomed the Duke and Duchess of Windsor and nearly every highness, lord, and honorable who set foot within the Los Angeles city limits. Mingling with the

Mary Pickford brings a little ray of sunshine to a desponding friend.

A scene from *The Taming of the Shrew,* with the Pickford-Fairbanks team

mighty were assorted famous colleagues—producers and directors and such top stars as Charlie Chaplin, John Barrymore, and Marie Dressler. I could go on and on, but I think you get the idea.

Marion Davies was an equally brilliant and considerably more inventive hostess. With William Randolph Hearst's millions at her pretty fingertips, little Marion's parties took place in famous restaurants like the Coconut Grove at the Ambassador Hotel, in her colonial mansion by Santa Monica's shore, and at Hearst's elegant castle of San Simeon. While Mary Pickford's parties were often rather dignified affairs, Marion's emphasized the spirit of mischief and fun that was so much a part of her own character. All those who knew her *when* speak about her with affection and a certain amount of respect. She had learned the secret of success—she was a warm and interested listener. In my estimation, she had a lot of acting ability, too. If Hearst hadn't insisted on presenting her as a pure, sweet, virginal heroine in all the pictures he sponsored for her, I am positive that she would have been one of our best comediennes. You could see that in films like *Page Miss Glory,* a later Davies vehicle, and you could even catch it in my favorite Davies movie, *Peg o' My Heart.*

Among the many blasts that Marion threw, I can recall hearing about a St. Patrick's Day affair, in which an entire restaurant was trimmed in green and white and expensive favors went to all the guests. On another occasion, Marion turned the Coconut Grove into a German beer garden and supplied Tyrolean peasant costumes for her guests. She loved costume balls. John Barrymore was slated to attend one of these affairs shortly after his arrival in Hollywood. He did not appear, but an old begging hobo did—and made himself such a nuisance that he was about to be thrown out before he managed to identify himself as the Great Profile. In addition to her glittering fêtes, Marion also gave informal every-Sunday-night buffets that climaxed a day's swimming in her pool or in the ocean at her Santa Monica estate. While we're on the subject of Marion Davies, I would also like to mention another party

Marion Davies sets out bravely in *Peg o' My Heart*. Her dog looks doubtful.

Marion of the movies: William Randolph Hearst put her name in lights.

she gave for some 2,000 poor children. This one took place on the MGM lot a few days before Christmas, and when it was over, each child received a basket in which there was a turkey with all the trimmings!

I would like to say a lot more about Marion's many charities but I haven't the space, so I'll sum it up by telling you that Hollywood's top party girl was also one of its top citizens—at least in my book!

And what would my book—or a Hollywood buffet—be without some California hors d'oeuvres?

CALIFORNIA HORS D'OEUVRES

1. 1 8-oz. carton cottage cheese
   juice of 1 orange
   ½ tsp. ground ginger

   In a large bowl put cottage cheese, orange juice, and ginger. With an electric mixer at high speed mix until all blended. Spread on thin strips of enriched white bread.

2. 1 8-oz. carton cottage cheese
   1 tsp. cinnamon

   Blend and serve on white bread strips.

3. 1 8-oz. carton cottage cheese
   ½ tbsp. curry powder
   5 strips bacon, crumbled

   With large spoon, stir until well blended and mashed. Spread on thin strips of garlic-buttered wholewheat bread.

4. 1 8-oz. carton cottage cheese
½ package pitted dates,
cut in small pieces

Mix dates and cottage cheese together, spread on white bread strips.

5. 3 ripe avocados
½ cup catsup
¼ cup mayonnaise

Remove seeds from avocados, mash with catsup and mayonnaise. Stir. Spread on melba rounds.

6. caviar (as much as you need)
lemon juice
chopped onion

Mix together caviar, juice, and onion. Serve on melba rounds.

7. 1 can tuna fish
(size depends on number of guests)
cottage cheese
soy sauce

Blend together tuna, cheese, and soy sauce. Serve on thin strips of buttered rye bread.

8. 1 cantaloupe
peperoni sausage

Cube melon. Cut sausage in thin slices and affix 1 slice to each cube with toothpick.

9. canned pineapple chunks
maraschino cherries
cream cheese

On any type of bread (raisin is recommended) spread cream cheese as a base. With a toothpick attach a pineapple chunk topped by half a cherry.

10. charcoal-broiled frankfurters
attached to toothpicks

11. shrimp
soy sauce

Soak shrimp in soy sauce for ½ hour. Remove and broil. Serve on toothpicks.

12. bleu cheese
sardines
pickled onions

Spread cheese on melba rounds. Mash sardines and add. Top with onion secured by toothpick.

For those buffet suppers, Marion always served a salad:

SALMON SALAD SUPREME

2 heads iceberg lettuce, chopped
2 bunches green onions, cut in small pieces
2 green peppers, diced
4 large ripe tomatoes, quartered or sliced
2 bunches watercress, separated and chopped
2 avocados, cut in small pieces
2 endives, sliced (optional)
1 cucumber, sliced
1 bottle catsup
1 small jar mayonnaise
1 16-oz. carton cottage cheese
1 small jar sweet mixed pickles
1 package chopped walnuts
2 large cans salmon
6 hard-boiled eggs, halved and dusted with paprika

Put prepared vegetables in large salad bowl. In another large bowl mix catsup, mayonnaise, cottage cheese, pickles, walnuts, and salmon. See that they are well mixed before adding to vegetables. Top with hard-boiled eggs. Chill for 2 hours before serving. (Serves 12–14)

CALIFORNIA FRUIT SALAD

3 fresh peaches
1 carton fresh strawberries
1 fresh coconut
1 bunch Thompson seedless grapes
1 bunch Concord grapes
1 cantaloupe
1 can pineapple chunks
1 can apricot halves
1 jar mayonnaise
½ bottle catsup
¼ jar honey
lettuce leaves

Slice peaches, strawberries. Chop coconut in small pieces, save milk. Pick grapes from stems, cut cantaloupe in chunks or balls. Drain cans of pineapple and apricots. Mix all prepared fruits and coconut together. In another bowl mix mayonnaise, catsup, honey, and coconut milk. Pour over salad, arrange on lettuce leaves, chill and serve. (Serves 8–10)

SOLE MARION

10 sole filets
½ bottle Marsala
salt and pepper, to taste

Rub both sides of filets with salt and pepper. Place in Teflon pan and fry for about 2 minutes on each side. Add wine to cover and cook for about 3 more minutes. (Serves 6)

BEEF STROGANOFF

3 lbs. round steak, cut into 1-inch strips
¼ lb. butter
2 cups chopped onions
1 clove garlic, minced
1 lb. fresh mushrooms, sliced
1 tsp. salt
¼ tsp. pepper
1 can beef bouillon, undiluted
1¾ cups sour cream

In a Dutch oven, melt ⅛ lb. butter. When melted, add some of the beef strips. Brown and remove with tongs. Add more beef until browned on both sides but rare. Set beef aside. In the same pot put the rest of the butter, onions, and mushrooms. Fry onion and garlic until they are a golden color. Add bouillon and stir until it comes to a boil. Lower the heat and add sour cream and then beef. Simmer until sauce and beef are hot.

Serve on egg noodles or on rice. (Serves 4–6)

INDIAN PUNCH

1 bottle (4/5 quart) gin
3½ cups pineapple juice
3½ cups grapefruit juice
½ lemon, sliced thin
1 orange, sliced thin
10 maraschino cherries, slivered
red vegetable coloring

Combine all ingredients. Add enough red coloring to turn mixture the color of pink lemonade. Serve with plenty of ice cubes.

CHAMPAGNE PUNCH

1 tsp. sugar syrup*
6 thin slices orange
6 thin slices lemon
1 tbsp. grated lemon rind
1 tbsp. grated orange rind
1 quart fresh strawberries
1 tsp. Angostura bitters
2 oz. brandy
2 oz. maraschino cherry juice
2 oz. white curaçao
1 oz. sherry
1 quart champagne
1 quart carbonated water

Mix all of the above ingredients in a large punch bowl. Add plenty of ice. Makes 3–4 quarts.

** Note: Sugar syrup is made by boiling equal parts of sugar and water together for 10 minutes.*

Shooting a film away from Hollywood was a wild adventure in the early days. We'll travel to the South Seas with Dolores Del Rio and share her recipe for Baked Bananas. Out West, Ken Maynard reveals the secret ingredients of his Western Steak, and in northern India with Frank Buck, we'll find a delicious souvenir to bring back: Vegetable Curry.

☆

CHAPTER 4 ON LOCATION

☆

When movies were movies, they really made some big pictures. I'm thinking about extravaganzas like *The Sign of the Cross,* the DeMille spectacular that starred Frederic March, Elissa Landi, and Claudette Colbert. Will you ever forget Charles Laughton as Nero? That was a re-creation of ancient Rome, but as far as I know its "cast of thousands" never set foot off the Paramount lot. And I have the impression that most of *Ben Hur* was filmed in Culver City. When John Barrymore did *The Sea Beast,* the crew didn't get much farther than San Pedro. Westerns were not at home on the ranges of Montana, Arizona, or Nevada. They were usually shot at Chatsworth, a few miles out of Hollywood.

When I was about eight, I went to Hollywood with my parents, and one of the high points of the trip was a visit to MGM in Culver City. Once inside, I was escorted around by a guide and I saw the great sound stages with all the lights, and outside, what do you suppose I ran into? A whole row of white wooden houses with fresh green lawns, each with a sprinkler playing on it. I got permission to go inside one of these houses, and to go inside was to emerge outside through a door that led nowhere—except to some tall timbers that were holding up the facades. There were other parts of Culver City that looked like a bombed-out French village. Later that afternoon I saw a whole ship, complete with rigging, sailing across an empty lot! Something that really fascinated me was a big tar pit I saw in Mar Vista, a place some three miles beyond Culver City. In this pit, you could see thrones and pillars and parts of rooms, all pure white plaster-of-Paris. No, they weren't rising prehistoric cities. They were sinking MGM sets, because that's where the studios dumped their junk—into the tar. I remember finding a large windowseat covered in white-quilted satin. I wanted to sit on it, but my mother vetoed the idea; she was afraid I'd get caught in the tar. That pit looked like a creation of Salvador Dali!

If you're wondering why I'm going on about all this, I'll tell you. I happen to have a lot of friends who have gone on location with movie companies, and they really had a ball. But that was later, when it didn't take eighteen hours to cross the country by plane and five days by ship across the Atlantic. However, I do have a few anecdotes and recipes about those intrepid camera crews who made it out of Los Angeles.

One of the best organized of the Hollywood explorers was a man who was a pro long before he ever set foot in a studio. I'm talking about "Bring 'em back alive" Frank Buck. To make his picture *Fang and Claw* he took with him Ray Taylor, his director, and Nick Cavalieri, who doubled as assistant director and chief cameraman. Also with them were Harry Squire, another cameraman, and J. A. Naulty, the business manager. With them, too, went 150 pieces of luggage and five cameras. And Buck had his two trusted guides Ali and Ahmed, not to mention fifty beaters and hunters. They tramped through the jungles on the Malay Peninsula and in northern India and brought back 100,000 feet of film, which were cut down to 10,000 for the movie.

According to Taylor, everything went without a hitch. "I never saw such organization," he commented. "We even had fresh vegetables and fruits to eat."

Did they bring back any live recipes? Why do you suppose I included them in this chapter? Don't worry—there's curry.

"Bring 'em back alive" Buck made his way in the world of fang and claw.

VEGETABLE CURRY

1 cup minced onions
1 cup sliced carrots
1 cup diced celery
1 cup shelled lima beans
1 cup shelled peas
¾ tsp. curry powder
¼ tsp. salt
⅛ tsp. turmeric
4 tbsp. butter
2 tsp. Worcestershire sauce
½ cup rice
(use one of the quick rices)
4 tbsp. chutney
4 tbsp. shredded coconut

In heavy saucepan put vegetables and enough boiling water to cover. Cook 10 minutes or until tender but still firm. Add curry powder, salt, turmeric, butter, and Worcestershire sauce. Prepare quick rice. Make a ring of rice and set steaming hot vegetables in center. Serve with chutney and coconut. (Serves 4)

SALMON CURRY

1 tbsp. olive oil
1 medium onion
1 can salmon
1 can tomato sauce
1 package almonds
1 tbsp. curry
¼ cup water

Heat oil in Dutch oven. Add onion and brown. Remove from flame. Add salmon, tomato sauce, almonds, curry, and water. Simmer until thick. Serve on rice. (Serves 4)

CURRIED LAMB

1½ lbs. lean lamb, cubed
2 tbsp. butter
3 small onions, minced
1 tbsp. curry
1 clove garlic
1 green apple, chopped
3 tomatoes, chopped
½ cup raisins
2 cups chicken broth
1 tsp. salt
⅛ tsp. white pepper
3 tbsp. flour

In large iron skillet, melt butter. Add lamb and onions. Sauté 5 minutes. Add curry, garlic, apple, tomatoes, and raisins. Add broth and seasoning. Stir. Cover and simmer for 1 hour. Remove lamb from pot and keep hot over steam. Strain sauce in pot through coarse sieve. Mix flour with a little water and add this paste to sauce. Stir until mixed. Cook 5 minutes, stirring constantly. Return lamb to sauce, heat. Serve with rice and side dishes of shredded coconut, peanuts, and chutney. (Serves 4–6)

MALAYAN STEAK

½ tsp. chili powder
10 almonds, chopped
3 tbsp. grated lemon rind
1 tsp. powdered ginger
⅛ tsp. turmeric
3 onions, chopped
4 cloves garlic, finely chopped
3 lbs. round steak, cut into 1-inch cubes
¼ lb. butter
2 cups boiling water
1 tsp. brown sugar
2 tsp. salt
4 tbsp. lemon juice
3 tbsp. plum jam

Combine chili powder, almonds, lemon rind, ginger, turmeric, onions, and garlic, and mix well. Roll steak pieces in mixture. Melt butter in saucepan. Add meat and cook over high flame for 5 minutes, stirring. Combine water, sugar, salt, lemon juice, and jam. Add to meat, mix well. Cook over low heat for 15 minutes. Stir occasionally. Serve with boiled rice. Pour sauce over meat and rice. (Serves 4–6)

The Last Days of Pompeii, made in 1935, was filmed at about the time that my mother was finally allowing me to see movies. Even though I was so young, I still remember Preston Foster as the gladiator. I also remember the last moments of the picture when everything seemed to come apart at once, including the theater—or so it sounded. That picture had one of the first of those great cataclysmic scenes with sound. There were also the earthquake in *San Francisco* and the great fire of *In Old Chicago,* but I guess I was impressed the most by Pompeii.

The background shots of Pompeii were made in Italy—and the producer, Merian C. Cooper, visited the ruins to do further research. He came back with some very good ideas and also some delicious Italian meals under his belt. I met Cooper, and he told me he still remembers a mussel dinner he had at a café down on the waterfront—the Bay of Naples, to you.

What the well-dressed gladiator will wear. Preston Foster in *Pompeii*

MUSSELS MARINIERE

3 quarts mussels in shells
1 cup dry white wine
1 tsp. minced shallots
1 tsp. parsley
dash of cayenne
1 tbsp. butter
more parsley, butter, and cayenne

Mussels should be ocean-fresh, heavy, shells tightly closed. Wash thoroughly, scraping shells with a knife; change water at least four times. Place in saucepan with wine, shallots, parsley, cayenne, and butter. Cover tightly and steam until shells open; take care that mussels are not overdone. Drain (reserve liquor). Remove empty shells, retaining only those with flesh on them. Arrange in serving dish and keep warm. Pour remaining liquid in a saucepan. Boil down to ¾ cup. Add butter, and cayenne, and pour over mussels. Sprinkle with parsley and serve hot. (Serves 6)

ITALIAN SALAD

1 head lettuce
¼ cup olive oil
⅛ cup vinegar
1 tsp. sugar
dash of salt

Chop lettuce. Combine oil, vinegar, sugar, and salt. Mix. Pour on salad. Toss. Chill before serving. (Serves 2–4)

You can't go to Italy without having spaghetti at least once!

MUSHROOM AND OLIVE SPAGHETTI

1 onion, minced
2 tbsp. olive oil
1 No. 2 can tomatoes
1 tsp. sugar
¼ tsp. salt
⅛ tsp. pepper
1 can cream of mushroom soup, undiluted
½ cup sliced stuffed olives
1 8-oz. package spaghetti
¼ cup grated cheese
¼ cup buttered crumbs
several slices American cheese

Cook onion in oil until it turns golden. Add tomatoes and seasonings. Simmer 15 minutes. Combine with soup and olives. Cook spaghetti in boiling salted water (according to directions on package). Grease baking dish and arrange spaghetti and sauce in alternate layers. Top with grated cheese and crumbs and add cheese slices. Bake in moderate oven (350°) 20–30 minutes. (Serves 4–6)

ZABAGLIONE

6 egg yolks
3 tbsp. sugar
⅓ cup Marsala

Put egg yolks in top of a double boiler. Add sugar and beat until mixture turns a light yellow. Let water in double boiler simmer, but don't let it come to a boil or mixture will set. Continue beating egg mixture and add wine gradually. Beat for 5–8 minutes until mixture thickens. Pour into dessert glasses and serve immediately. (Serves 2–4)

Now let's go on to another location—far, far north, where MGM sent its crews to make *Eskimo,* and where Universal, also Eskimo-minded, shot most of the picture *S.O.S. Iceberg.* While nothing untoward happened to the MGM expedition, the Universal camera staff found itself standing on an iceberg in the middle of the Arctic Sea, just when the spring thaw set in. The berg parted and tipped the crew into the chilly waters, whence it was rescued by some helpful Eskimos, who probably did not want to lose their wages as extras.

In case you're wondering what whale meat tastes like, I am not giving you any recipes—but if you're very curious, you can go to a gourmet grocery and buy it in cans. I'm going to cop out and offer you two frosty versions of a great dessert.

FRANKLIN'S BAKED ALASKA

4 egg whites
1 cup powdered sugar
1 pound cake
1-quart brick ice cream

Beat egg whites and ¾ cup sugar together until light and dry. Cut top off pound cake—lengthwise. Cover baking sheet with tinfoil. Put cake on baking sheet and put ice cream on cake—cake should be longer on all sides than ice cream. Cover ice cream with thick coating of meringue, dust with remaining powdered sugar. Place in hot oven (400°) and brown for about 3 minutes. (Serves 2–4)

BLACK-AND-WHITE BAKED ALASKA

1 frozen ice-cream chocolate roll
2 egg whites
2 tbsp. sugar

Place roll on baking sheet. Cover completely with beaten egg whites mixed with sugar. Brown in hot oven (450°) for 3 minutes. Serve, sprinkle with chocolate chips. (Serves 2–4)

From the frozen North, let's wander back to the sunny South Seas. It was here that Dolores Del Rio and Joel McCrea made *Bird of Paradise,* and here that the intrepid traveler Douglas Fairbanks, Sr., shot *Mr. Robinson Crusoe.* As a kid, I liked *Crusoe* better. In *Bird of Paradise,* the lovely Miss Del Rio ended up throwing herself into a volcano. I never did like waste.

Bananas anyone?

BAKED BANANAS

1 dozen bananas, peeled
3 tbsp. butter
4 tbsp. lemon juice
7 tbsp. sugar
½ tsp. salt

Place bananas in one layer in baking dish. Place bowl in pan of warm water, and in bowl put butter, lemon juice, sugar, and salt. Stir until butter is melted. Pour over bananas. Bake 30 minutes, at 350°, basting often with liquid. (Serves 4–6)

BAKED BANANAS 2

4 bananas, peeled and cut lengthwise
lemon juice
sugar
chopped almonds
chopped pecans

Place banana halves in buttered baking dish. Sprinkle with lemon juice. Bake 15 minutes in moderate oven (350°), without reducing heat, sprinkle with sugar, and bake 5 more minutes. Just before serving, sprinkle with nuts. (Serves 2–4)

Joel McCrea, before he traded in his suit and tie for chaps and spurs

BANANA LOAF

⅔ cup sugar
⅓ cup butter
2 eggs
3 ripe bananas
1 tsp. vanilla

sift together:
2 tsp. baking powder
¼ tsp. soda
1 tsp. salt
2 cups flour

Cream together butter and sugar until light. Add one egg, beat. Add another egg, beat. Mash bananas with potato masher and add to shortening mixture. Add vanilla. Add flour mixture a little at a time, beating constantly. Pour into loaf pan (8 inches x 4 inches). Bake in moderate oven (350°) for 50 minutes. Cool. Slice.

As I have mentioned, most Western movies were made in Chatsworth, California—an area noted for its amazing rock formations. As it happens, I followed one of those famous wagon-trains as 't wended its way out to that territory. The film being shot was a Columbia Pictures B-movie entitled *Adventures in Silverado,* based on a story by Robert Louis Stevenson.

I spent a day out there among chuck wagons, portable dressing rooms, and actors. I did not see any action, because waiting to greet us when we arrived was a high wind that did not desist all day. Still, I have some pretty pungent memories of the place—of

Even under that black hat, Ken Maynard is really one of the good guys.

stage mothers, waiting for the wagons to roll and putting their ragged-costumed offspring into positions where the cameras could catch their grinning, freckled faces, of Forrest Tucker and Edgar Barrier playing poker all day in a portable dressing room, of the wagon drivers, hairdressers, and makeup men off by themselves chatting about wives, families, and new automobiles they planned to buy, of the one-armed bandits that mysteriously made their appearances on the backs of wagons, of the cursing camera crew glaring at the dust-filled atmosphere. As for the food, well, it was chicken sandwiches packed in lunchboxes at the Columbia commissary.

As I understand it, the crews that used to go with that one-time circus-rodeo-rider-turned-Western-star, Ken Maynard, had it better. Maynard took a real-live chuck wagon along with him on location and used to dispense a lot of Western specialties. His staple was steak, cooked or raw.

WESTERN STEAK

4 club steaks
charcoal seasoning
salt
pepper
lemon juice

Before broiling, coat steaks in charcoal seasoning, salt, pepper, and lemon juice. Broil to your preference. (Serves 4)

HAMBURGERS ON THE RANGE

1 egg
1 lb. chopped sirloin
1 onion, chopped
1/8 tsp. garlic powder
1/4 tsp. salt
1/8 tsp. pepper
juice of 1/2 lemon
1/2 tsp. bacon bits

Mix together raw egg and sirloin until egg is completely blended. Add onion, garlic powder, salt, pepper, lemon juice, and bacon bits. Mix thoroughly. Serve raw, on bread or toast. (Serves 2–4)

CAMPFIRE MEATBALLS

¾ lb. chopped sirloin
¼ lb. chopped pork
1 egg
1 medium onion, chopped
1 clove garlic, minced
¼ cup catsup (optional)
salt and pepper to taste
1 cup seasoned breadcrumbs

Mix together meats and raw egg. Add onion, garlic, catsup, salt, and pepper. Roll in seasoned breadcrumbs. Fry in Teflon pan until well done, turning to brown on both sides. (Serves 2–4)

Have you ever eaten potatoes over a campfire—you know, shoved them on forks and roasted them until they were done? Ummmm, good! Well, not everyone has a campfire handy, so this recipe is for oven-baked potatoes, with shrimps, yet.

SHRIMP BOATS

4 medium-to-large baking potatoes
½ pint carton sour cream
½ cup brine shrimps, canned
1 tbsp. chopped chives
½ tsp. salt
⅛ tsp. pepper
⅛ tsp. paprika
4 tbsp. butter

Bake potatoes in hot oven (400°) for 1 hour. Meanwhile blend sour cream, shrimps, chives, and seasonings. When potatoes are done, remove from oven, split, add 1 tbsp. butter and ¼ shrimp mix to each. Return to oven for 5 minutes. (Serves 4)

Even if we didn't make it to Texas, here is a salad that did—a real regional favorite:

LONE STAR SALAD

2 cups cottage cheese
1 green pepper, finely chopped
1 small onion, finely chopped
salt
6 tomatoes
French dressing
paprika
1 head iceberg lettuce

Combine cheese, green pepper, and onion. Season with salt to taste. Cut each tomato in sixths almost to blossom end. Spread apart enough to insert cheese-onion mix. Cover with French dressing and a little paprika. Serve on lettuce. (Serves 6)

Another star who made a great many Westerns was that strong, silent he-man, Richard Dix. Before I get to the food, I'd like to

Richard Dix, star of the Western *Yellow Dust,* here with Edith Fellows

tell you a little story I know about Dix. He was starring in *Cimarron,* which dealt with the land-rush to Oklahoma. One scene in particular was a big deal. All the covered wagons were lined up at a starting point. There were hundreds of them, filled with men, women, and children, and drawn by horses and oxen. Dix, as the star, was not in this particular sequence. But just as things got on the move, Dix, watching from the sidelines, saw a little boy fall out of one of the wagons. There was no way to halt the shooting. Dix flung himself on his horse and, riding over to the little boy, pulled him out of danger, tossed him in a wagon, and then joined the other riders in the scene while the cameras continued to roll. Dix, unlike many of his colleagues, was a

Dix and Ann Harding, on location for a shoot-em-up called *The Conquerors*

stickler for authenticity. Every time he did a Western, he read up on the historical background of the action, and generally, he liked to shoot his films on "the scene of the crime," as it were. I happen to know that when he made *Yellow Dust,* which had to do with the discovery of gold in California, he insisted that the company set up headquarters in Kern River Valley, near the original site. As it happened, it was a great idea because the Sierra Nevada range figured prominently in the scenes and formed a magnificent natural background for the movie.

I wish I'd been old enough to go along, because I'm told that Dix treated the crew to a big barbecue when the shooting was finished. I am including a few barbecue sauces for the meat, which should be cooked over a bed of charcoal.

BARBECUE MARINADE

4 cups red-wine vinegar
1 quart Chianti
1 tsp. thyme leaves
12 sprigs parsley
2 bay leaves
4 shallots, cut in half
2 medium-sized carrots, sliced
1 large onion, minced
2 cloves garlic, bruised
1 tbsp. salt
12 peppercorns, bruised

Mix above ingredients. Take 4–6-lb. cut of beef. Place in earthenware dish and cover with marinade. Leave in refrigerator for about 5 days, turning each day.

WESTERN BEEF SAUCE

1 tbsp. butter
¼ cup each minced onion and celery, mixed
2 tbsp. brown sugar
2 tbsp. vinegar
1 tbsp. English mustard
2 tbsp. Worcestershire sauce
1 tbsp. beef tea
¼ tsp. salt
dash of cayenne
1 cup tomato catsup
1 cup hot water
1 tbsp. lemon juice

Melt butter in saucepan. Add onion and celery mixture. Cook over low flame for 10 minutes. Add everything except lemon juice. Stir over medium flame until sauce thickens. Just before removing from heat, add lemon juice.

HOT AND SPICY SAUCE

½ cup water
½ cup tomato catsup
2 tbsp. India relish
1 tbsp. cider vinegar
1 tbsp. Worcestershire sauce
1 medium onion, chopped
1 tsp. salt
½ tsp. paprika
½ tsp. chili powder
¼ tsp. black pepper
¼ tsp. red pepper

Mix water, catsup, India relish, vinegar, and Worcesteshire sauce. Add onion. Simmer 5 minutes, over low flame. Mix spices and salt. Add enough of the other hot liquid to form paste Continue adding liquid until spices are creamy. Add rest of liquid and simmer 10 minutes. Keep hot in top of double boiler until ready to use. Serve with barbecued lamb or salmon, for a delicious and different cookout!

Boris Karloff and Bela Lugosi, in a spine-tingling scene inspired by Poe

They didn't try to devour Cleveland! Boris Karloff, Lon Chaney, and Frederic March haunted the kitchen as well as the set. Bela Lugosi was no slouch, either—try his Hungarian specialty, Chicken Paprikash.

☆

CHAPTER 5 WHEN MONSTERS WERE MONSTERS

☆

While camera crews were sent all over the globe to film some of those early Hollywood extravaganzas, many of the most exciting movies were shot right at home. In fact California was the location for every one of the movies that thrill me most —the thrillers. Few modern-day horror movies can compare with those early films. Monsters were really monsters in those days and they didn't kid around!

They went no further than the nearest mortuary to film *Dracula,* which starred Bela Lugosi, a man strictly from Hungary. Bela Lugosi was justifiably proud of his culinary specialties, which were strictly from Hungary, too.

CHICKEN PAPRIKASH

½ cup flour
1 tsp. paprika
½ tsp. salt
¼ tsp. white pepper
1 broiling chicken (3½ lbs.)
1 tbsp. bacon drippings
1 tbsp. butter
1 large onion, minced
1 tbsp. paprika
½ cup hot water
2 tbsp. flour
2 cups sour cream

Blend flour, paprika, salt, pepper; pour into paper bag. Drop chicken into bag, a piece at a time, shake well until each piece is coated. Melt bacon fat and butter in heavy skillet over high heat; brown chicken in fat and fry on each side 3 minutes; push to one side of skillet, making room to brown onion for 3 more minutes; sprinkle 1 tbsp. paprika over chicken; add hot water, cover skillet, turn down heat. Simmer gently for 45 minutes. Turn chicken pieces every so often to avoid sticking; add a small quantity of water if chicken is not moist enough to prevent burning. When chicken is tender, remove from skillet, keep hot over steam. Quickly add 2 tbsp. flour to pan gravy, blend; when smooth, add sour cream, stir constantly for 5 minutes. Cover, simmer gently for 5 more minutes. Replace chicken pieces. Serve with egg noodles or cooked rice. (Serves 4)

For the exorcise: Edward van Sloan really knows how to hurt a vampire.

ZUCCHINI PAPRIKA

1 lb. zucchini squash
1 cup flour
1 tsp. garlic salt
1 tsp. paprika
½ tsp. pepper
1 cup milk
butter or margarine
additional paprika

Wash zucchini. Slice into small disks. Blend flour, garlic salt, paprika, and pepper in bowl. Dip zucchini disks into milk and then into flour mixture. Fry in deep, hot butter (375°) for 2 minutes. Drain on paper towels. Sprinkle more paprika lightly over slices. (Serves 2–4)

Just for the record and while I am reminded of it, here is my own recipe for zucchini. It's as Hungarian as I am, which means about one-eighth.

FRANKLIN'S ZUCCHINI

4 or 5 long, hard zucchini squash
mushrooms (optional)
¼ lb. butter
salt and pepper

Slice zucchini very thin (you should almost be able to see through each disk). Slice mushrooms very thin. In a large iron skillet melt butter. Season to taste. Sauté zucchini until almost black. (Serves 2–4)

Talking about Bela Lugosi, it's a tribute to his talent that his name is so identified with creepy creatures. Offstage, Bela was suave and charming. You would never have known that he did so much of his emoting in a coffin.

While I'm in the mood, I think I'll tell you a little about Lon Chaney, Frederic March, and Boris Karloff. When they were making the early monster movies, they put a lot into them—good acting and, as Churchill would say, blood, sweat, and tears. The last three ingredients were supplied by those actors who dressed up in scare costumes.

Lon Chaney portrayed a great many of life's unfortunates, and by the time he got through with the chemicals and the greasepaint, he was even more unfortunate. He risked a hernia crawling around in his Quasimodo get-up. In *The Road to Mandalay,* he was required to be blind in one eye. For this part he obtained the effect by using a chemical so strong it could be employed for only two hours at a time. That's called taking your role seriously, and he did. He never liked to be photographed because he wanted the public to remember him only as he appeared on the screen. There used to be a popular joke around Hollywood that went "Don't step on it—it might be Lon Chaney."

You hardly ever think of handsome Frederic March as a monster. He won most of his fame portraying Anthony Adverse, or Robert Browning in *The Barretts of Wimpole Street,* and many other great parts, including his roles in *Death of a Salesman* and

Middle of the Night, in which he aged so gracefully. Did you ever see him playing the title role in *Death Takes a Holiday?* That was, as they now say, a beautiful picture, in the sense that it was highly artistic and compelling. Even in his shadow costume March was not in the least frightening. And about that shadow costume: If you saw the film you probably wondered how they managed that effect in which you could see right through Mr. March. Well, it was done with mirrors. In each scene where the shadow appeared, there was a duplicate set with a mirror that projected his image moving through the furniture. It was a very complicated setup, and I don't think I have described it quite right. They shot a lot of takes on those scenes, and finally, after the twenty-fourth time around, March got mad. He waited until the take had been shot, and then he moved into the duplicate room, smashing the mirrors. "You'll have to print it the way it is," he told the director. "Fortunately it was perfect."

March's other excursion into the macabre was as *Dr. Jekyll and Mr. Hyde,* in the version directed by Rouben Mamoulian.

The suave Frederic March

That was a real pain in the neck, eye, back, and so on—for the actor. He told me all about it. "Mamoulian," says March, "decided that the character of Hyde should be more ape than man. He believed that the personification of evil should be evil in appearance. He had to be covered with hair, snarling and gulping like an insane animal, making uncouth noises in his throat; he had to have a low forehead, protruding teeth, and flaring nostrils."

Consequently Fred's head was built up into a cone shape, his mouth was stretched over a plate of false jagged teeth, his nose distorted to abnormal width, and his eyes pulled down by invisible tape. It hurt.

"My eyes gave me the real trouble," he explains, wincing in reminiscence. "It was real physical suffering; they pained me constantly and even when I wasn't wearing the makeup, I had a headache. But I did wear the makeup for twelve hours at a stretch—you see it was terribly complicated to apply. I was certainly glad when I finished that movie. I lost four pounds in the process."

Boris Karloff as himself. On the screen he was a fright for sore eyes.

An equally uncomfortable get-up was donned by Boris Karloff as the Frankenstein monster. He told me that it took him three hours to get into his monster suit. His boots alone weighed eighteen pounds each, and a lot of extra putty went onto his head. His forehead was knobbed to give the impression that several brains had been tried and found wanting before the good doctor slipped the right IQ into the skull cavity. As for that heavy-lidded look, his eyelids were waxed until he could scarcely lift them. All in all, the makeup weighed forty-eight pounds, and it not only caused severe physical discomfort to Karloff, but the

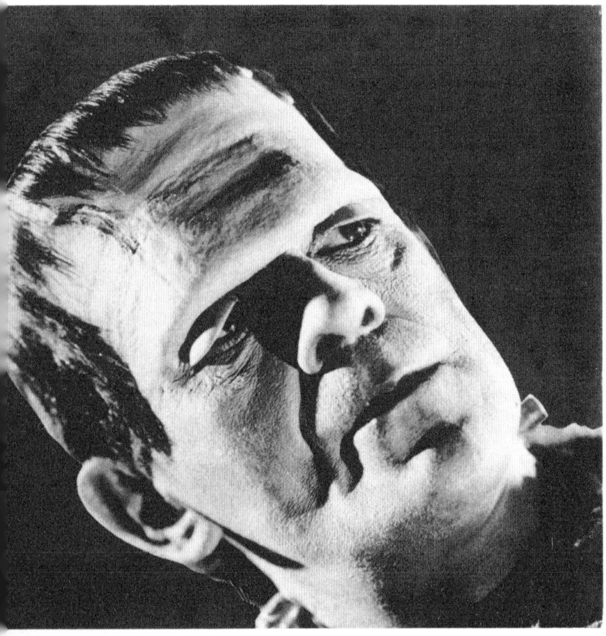

difficulty of applying it forced him to work harder. He bested the March record by being monstrous for eighteen and twenty-three hours at a stretch.

Karloff is credited with inventing the quick Hollywood diet. You want to know how? Dressed as Im-ho-tep, a mummy resurrected after 2,000 years of moldering in a tomb and therefore not looking quite as fit as he had when alive, he strode into the commissary at Universal to have lunch. While Karloff had no difficulty in eating, everybody else did, and when he finally looked up from his steak, he found the place almost deserted.

Karloff incarnations: left, as Dr. Frankenstein's monster and the Mad Doctor; center, the Mummy; and with Elsa Lanchester, the monster's bride

Top left, Charles Chaplin. Center, Charlie the tramp and Buster Keaton, as melancholy as any Hamlet. Bottom left, Laurel and Hardy look pleased.

The good old days of vaudeville inspired many an economical recipe. Fred Allen, Buster Keaton, Jack Benny—they all lived on the road, and it was a long hard road. Dishes like Mulligan Stew and Noodle Pie kept them going. Vaudeville comedy immortalized another specialty: Custard Pie.

☆

CHAPTER 6 HOT PLATE SPECIAL

☆

Acting is an uncertain profession. I know I'm not telling you anything new, but let me continue. I think breaking into pictures was even more difficult than making it big on Broadway. Oh, I know, I'm going to meet with arguments. I'm going to hear that Arleen Whelan was a manicurist, and Dorothy Lamour was an elevator operator, and all Lana Turner had to do was wear a sweater and drink a soda in Schwab's Drugstore. Then, of course, Norma Talmadge, a sweet young girl who had just graduated from high school, took her pictures to the old

Norma Talmadge and Colleen Moore: starlets who made it

Vitagraph studio and was immediately signed, while Colleen Moore, standing in an elevator, was jolted against D. W. Griffith and put on salary almost instantly. Sure, there are exceptions to every rule, but there are also a lot of photogenic panhandlers in Hollywood. And people going out to the West Coast in the old days were struck by the beauty of waitresses, maids, and shop clerks, and by the manly charm of every gardener. Maybe that's where all those handsome milkman and iceman jokes originated?

Getting back to my point, acting *is* an uncertain profession, and in the long run, it's experience that counts. Now, I'm going to be even more specific: those of you who've listened to my radio programs and viewed my TV shows know that I have a special penchant for comedians, for Buster Keaton, Harry Langdon, W. C. Fields, Jimmy Durante, Laurel and Hardy, Chaplin

Three funny men: The much put-upon Harry Langdon; Durante in his favored role as Jimmy the well-dressed man; W.C. Fields in a sober moment

—all of them. There's been a lot said about the tough conditions under which all those comedians had to work in Hollywood when Mack Sennett was putting on all those two-reelers. But compared with the kind of experiences they'd been having before they arrived on the Coast, they were doing their pratfalls in paradise. In case you're wondering what they'd been doing before their movies, I'm talking about vaudeville.

Today, the nostalgia-minded will talk about vaudeville with a sentimental sigh for the old two-a-day route. Most of the movies done with a vaudeville background end when the performer in question finally plays the Palace. Remember how misty-eyed everybody got when the late, lamented, and lovely Judy Garland played the Palace, not so many years back? That's because a lot of them remembered when the Palace was Mecca. But for every act that made it, there were hundreds on the road in tank towns that nobody except a theater manager ever heard of, towns that aren't even in existence any more. In fact, they were little more than a post-office address in the days when the local icehouse served as theater. R.F.D. Nowhere!

Vaudeville, in case any of you youngsters don't know what I mean, was a popular type of variety show that existed from 1875 to the mid-thirties, though Fred Allen would have it that it really came to an end in 1925. The word "vaudeville" was first applied to a variety show by H. J. Sargent. Sargent, turned out of one theater to make way for a French-imported variety entertainment, called his own variety show Vaudeville because it sounded French.

There was plenty of variety in a vaudeville show, too. Anywhere along the route, you'd find comedy teams, jugglers, magicians, dog, cat, horse, snake, elephant, lion, tiger, rabbit acts, belly dancers, ballet dancers (Pavlova and Nijinsky had an act), cello players (I will not list the types of instruments because there were too many, from harmonicas to musical brooms). In England, Ethel Barrymore traveled in vaudeville with a short one-acter, Sir

Jack Benny had eyes only for Joan Bennett in *Artists and Models Abroad.*

James Barrie's *The Twelve Pound Look,* which served her very well until the thirties, when English workingmen audiences resented the fact that a woman could pull down twelve pounds while they were starving. Sarah Bernhardt, wooden leg and all, hit the trail as Queen Elizabeth and the young L'Aiglon, when she was over sixty. Marie Dressler and Polly Moran teamed for a two-a-day after they'd made it big in movies. Jean Acker, the first Mrs. Rudolph Valentino, appeared in vaudeville. Jack Benny, shuddering from stage fright, had a comic turn with a silent fiddle, and a man called Freddy James, the World's Worst Juggler, was none other than that Benny nemesis, Fred Allen. W. C. Fields made his dry remarks and played his remarkable games of pool, while Annette Kellerman, the famous swimming star, climbed a ladder and leaped into another kind of pool right on stage. Other aquatic tricks were performed by the great escape artist Harry Houdini.

Indeed, there seemed to be no limit to what could and did happen on the stage. There were limits, however, and they had to do with what was said rather than what happened on stage. You couldn't tell any smutty jokes or use any profanity. Theater managers and sometimes their wives censored the material in comic acts, and some of their deletions are rather hard to understand these days. You couldn't say "slob," "feet," "socks," or "breath." Don't ask me why. On second thought, maybe I know why. Back in the era when vaudeville was really going great guns—in the nineties and for about a decade afterwards—even piano legs were called "limbs," and to protect the innocence of the kids who played on or under the instrument, those "limbs" often had skirts tied around them, as did chairs and tables.

Houdini, master escape artist

The inimitable Chaplin: On location, directing *The Gold Rush;* and with Jackie Coogan in *The Kid*

Blacklisting managers weren't the only hazards a vaudeville performer encountered on the road. I'm not talking about things like a swimming tank breaking and flooding the orchestra and the first rows, which did happen at least once. Nor do I mean the time one trainer's lion decided that he was hungry enough to eat the man standing in the wings, or the time the mice from a magic act fled into the audience. Some of the worst hazards vaudeville performers faced were the traveling conditions, which includes, of course, what they did and didn't eat. Those hardy comics who survived to make it big on Broadway or in the movies often tell stories about what the road was like, and from what some of them have told me, I'm glad I never traveled it. I've had it hard in my time too, but not like that. There are unions now—and those hard times are the reason.

Think about America back in the days when the railroad business was booming. Distances were long, then, and unpaved, too. You didn't roll off a superhighway onto an exit marked 12. You took a train—often several trains—to reach a town in which you were booked. Schedules were uncertain, and some luckless performers were liable to pack up after a night of performing, catch the train to the station where they were supposed to change for another iron horse, only to find that it had just puffed out of view. That didn't mean you piled into the nearest Howard Johnson's. In that era, hotel and boarding-house keepers did not cater to actors, whose finances they suspected, even when the performers were successful. They also complained that every time they rented to an actor, they lost towels, sheets, and anything else that wasn't nailed down. Consequently, a lot of performers spent the nights they didn't catch the train sleeping on the station-house floor, provided there was a station house. Furthermore, if a performer, through no fault of his own, missed the train and arrived late at the theater, his pay was docked.

Things weren't any easier for them in the big cities. Buster Keaton remembered how he and his father trudged from manager to manager through the icy streets of New York. By the time they were hired, they couldn't remember their last square meal. Talking about meals, I am dedicating this chapter to the folks who cooked dinner for an entire family of performers.

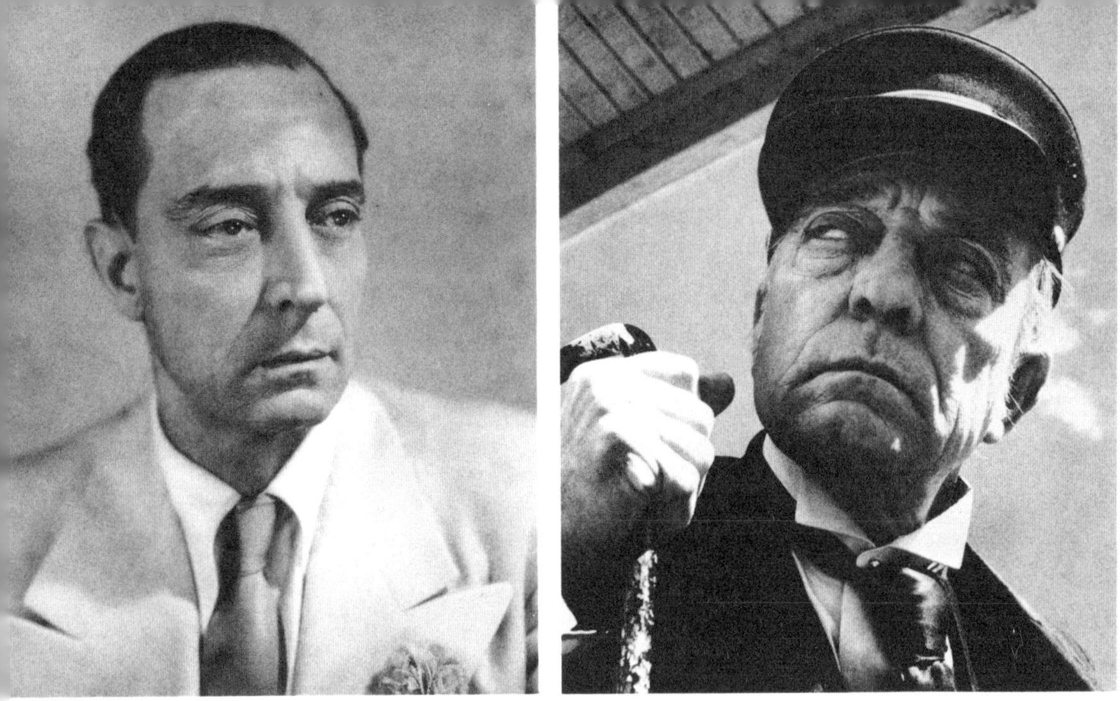

Buster Keaton was the train conductor in *Around the World in 80 Days.*

over a hot-plate in a windowless hall-bedroom, or in a tent by the side of the road, or backstage between acts. The recipes you will find here are designed to make the most of a little, and they'll give you a flavor of what it meant to scrimp and save and starve for art.

PINE FLOAT

toothpick
glass of water

You float the toothpick on the water.

Of course, I'm kidding. I don't know who made up the recipe for a pine float, but I bet it was one of those stranded comics I was telling you about.

THEME AND VARIATIONS—THE FRANKFURTER

1 package frankfurters
and any one of the following:
mustard
garlic
vinegar
relish
catsup
teriyaki sauce
soy sauce
garlic salt
cloves
onion salt

Split frankfurters and dab each side with any of the above ingredients. Practically anything tastes good on a frankfurter. Grill each side over an open flame or under a broiler.

SPINACH WITH BACON BITS

1 lb. spinach
1 slice onion
4 strips well-done bacon, crumbled
salt and pepper

Wash spinach and put in saucepan. Do not add extra water. Add onion, crumbled bacon, and salt and pepper. Cook until spinach is tender. (Serves 4–6)

LAMB STEW

2½ lbs. lamb shoulder, cut in small pieces, fat trimmed away
approx. ½ cup flour
4 tbsp. bacon drippings
5 cups water
6 white onions
6 carrots, split
1 large parsnip, cut in pieces
1 bay leaf
½ tsp. marjoram
2 cloves
pinch of thyme
6 potatoes, halved
2 tsp. salt
¼ tsp. white pepper

Roll meat in flour. Brown in bacon drippings. Put in stew pan and add water, vegetables (except potatoes) and spices. Cover, bring to boil. Reduce heat and simmer for 1½ hours. Add potatoes, salt, and pepper. Cook 25 minutes more. (Serves 6)

MULLIGAN STEW

1 soup bone
1 lb. stewing beef
6 quarts water
3 large onions
6 carrots

6 stalks celery
2 parsnips
2 tbsp. salt
½ tsp. pepper
1 can tomato soup

In stew pan put bone, beef, and water. Cook for 1 hour. Add vegetables and seasoning. Cook until vegetables are tender. Add soup and cook 3 more minutes. (Serves 6)

FLEMISH STEW

4 lbs. stewing beef
4 onions, chopped
¼ cup vinegar
1 tsp. brown sugar
½ tsp. marjoram
½ tsp. thyme
½ tsp. rosemary
1 bottle dark beer

Cut beef into small pieces, removing fat. Brown with onions. Add remaining ingredients and simmer for 2 hours. (Serves 6–8)

NOODLE PIE

1 package egg noodles
1 8-oz. carton cottage cheese
¼ cup milk
salt and pepper, to taste
1 package American cheese slices

Boil noodles according to directions on package. In a greased baking dish, mix noodles, cottage cheese, milk, salt, and pepper. Mix pieces of American cheese through dish and top with several slices. Put in moderate oven (350°) for about 25 minutes. (Serves 4–6)

MUSTARD GREENS WITH POTATOES

⅛ lb. salt pork
1½ quarts cold water
2 lbs. mustard greens
12 new potatoes

Slice salt pork very thin and put in saucepan. Add water. Cover and simmer for 1 hour. Meanwhile wash mustard greens, remove heads, and cut stalks into pieces. Clean and scrape potatoes. After salt pork has simmered for 1 hour, add stalks and simmer for 15 minutes. Add potatoes and mustard heads. Cook 20 minutes. (Serves 6–8)

TUNA SURPRISE

1 can tuna
1 can bean sprouts
1 can pineapple chunks
1 cup cooked rice (a quick rice will do)
½ cup soy sauce
¼ tsp. ginger

Combine tuna, bean sprouts, and pineapple chunks with pineapple juice. Heat. Cook rice according to directions on package and combine with first mixture. Add soy sauce to which ginger has been added. (Serves 4–6)

MASHED POTATOES

1 package mashed potato mix, with:
1 tbsp. sour cream with freeze-dried chives
or:
1 tbsp. bouillon
or:
1 tbsp. hot tomato juice with either Worcestershire sauce or melted butter to which ⅛ tsp. garlic powder has been added. (Serves 2–4)

Note: Potatoes were one of the great staples on the road. They had to do it the hard way, though; there were no quick mixes.

Did you ever hear the old ditty:

A peanut sat on the railroad track.
Its heart was all a-flutter.
The 6:45 was coming along.
Toot-toot—peanut butter.

Peanut butter might have been a tragic end for that particular peanut, but for many actors of my acquaintance, it was the one thing that kept them alive in the days when there was no money. It was filling, and if it was also fattening, you don't need to count calories when you're starving. So, when you see a jar of peanut butter in the store, buy it, take it home, spread it on bread and add some sort of jam, and you'll be eating like half the acting fraternity of yore.

I am always surprised when I let my mind wander back to the old days when the comics were wowing 'em in those two-reelers. Have you ever wondered why so many pictures were comedies? In those days, just like these, everybody could do with a little laughter—especially performers. In the early days of comedy, $50 a week was a good salary. When Charlie Chaplin began receiving $1,000 per week, everyone was utterly amazed. He deserved it. They all deserved a lot of money, because acting was a risk in many ways—all those falls the Keystone Kops took were for real. In fact, according to Buster Keaton, the boys got far too shook up. There was an art to falling, as Keaton knew. The way he put it, you had to protect both ends of your spine from the jarring it received. Talk about the hard way, Keaton knew every inch of it. He'd been on the stage in medicine shows and vaudeville since he was five years old, as one of the three Keatons, in what was termed a roughhouse act. His father, Joe Keaton, threw the kid

all over the stage, and if he hadn't been born with an acrobat's body and an instinctive sense of timing, he wouldn't have survived to become one of filmdom's greatest comics.

I could go on and on about those old, unrehearsed days, and about the marvelous art of Charlie Chaplin, Charlie Chase, Harold Lloyd, Harry Langdon, John Bunny, Laurel and Hardy, Fatty Arbuckle, Mabel Normand, and Louise Fazenda. But since you're probably getting hungry, I'll get down to cases—or rather pies. In that era, movies were very informal and there were very few shooting scripts. If you were Hal Roach or Mack Sennett, you took your comic, a girl, a car, and maybe a couple of other people and you went to a given spot and waited for something funny to

Their cinematic hijinks were never matched: Stan Laurel and Oliver Hardy.

inspire you. One day Mabel Normand watched Ben Turpin, of the famed crossed-eyes, while he worked. She thought he wasn't being quite funny enough, and she looked around to see what she could do. Opportunity in the shape of a custard pie someone was going to eat for lunch presented itself. She sent it skimming across the set to land squarely on Turpin's face. With his features framed in goo and his eyes trying to meet each other across his nose, he was a hilarious sight. He was also a landmark in comedy. From then on, the pie was as much a two-reeler prop as the car they used for the inevitable chase sequence at the end of the picture. The pie Mabel hurled was strictly an amateur affair. Those that later sailed across the scenes had special reinforced

Comedy heavyweight Fatty Arbuckle maintaining an untenable position

Great names in the annals of cust pie: Mabel Normand—she th it; Ben Turpin—he really caugh

bottom crusts. It was eventually decided that custard pies should be thrown at brunettes, while blondes suffered cherry pies—contrast counted.

It would have helped matters if the pastry cooks who prepared the daffy dough could have used the many pie-crust mixes you can find today. They couldn't, but you can, so I am not giving you any directions on how to make a pie crust. Consider that it is in the box you will buy.

CUSTARD PIE

(remember, suitable for throwing
only if you have enough crust)

4 eggs
6 tbsp. sugar
dash of salt
3 cups milk
1 tsp. vanilla
nutmeg

Beat eggs slightly, add sugar, salt, milk, and vanilla Stir until sugar is dissolved. Turn into the 9-inch pie shell you will have prepared, which is in the tinfoil pan you will have purchased. Pie shell should be brushed with egg white to prevent soaking. Dust custard-mixture with nutmeg and bake in hot oven (450°) for 10 minutes. Lower heat to 350° and bake for 30 minutes more. Eat or throw.

Mr. Show Business himself, Al Jolson made *The Jazz Singer* a milestone.

A few names will live forever in Memory Lane, like Eddie Cantor and an era we'll never forget. (Try his borscht—you won't forget that, either.) Reminisce with Rudy Vallee over his chilled Ceviche, then walk up Broadway with Mr. Show Business—Al Jolson—for a Hot Pastrami Sandwich and a last long look down Memory Lane.

☆

CHAPTER 7 CURTAIN CALL

☆

I suppose that during the course of my years in radio and television, I have met about everybody there is to know in the business, including many of the old-timers who thrilled me when I was little. However, I am dedicating this chapter to just four of them—Eddie Cantor, Al Jolson, Paul Whiteman, and Rudy Vallee. By no coincidence, all of them had or have musical connections, and music was my own ticket to the big time.

When I was fourteen or fifteen, I got a radio job with Martin Block, picking records for his famous *Make-Believe Ballroom.*

Paul Whiteman, star of *King of Jazz,* played himself in *Strike Up the Band.*

I used to spend all the time I wasn't doing my high-school homework going through *Billboard* and *Cashbox,* picking what I thought would be the big hits of the hour. It turned out that I had a sort of telepathic perception—maybe because as a Pisces, I'm slightly psychic (actually I don't dig astrology, much). Anyhow, whatever I picked, I was seldom wrong. Well, Paul was starting the Paul Whiteman Record Club, the first coast-to-coast disk jockey show in radio, and having heard about my uncanny perception, he called me over and gave me a job picking records for him. That was how I got my start. I guess I was one of his last protégés. He had had many, you know—Bing Crosby, Dinah Shore, Tommy and Jimmy Dorsey, Hoagy Carmichael. Did I ever have dinner with Paul? Countless times. He was quite thin when I knew him. At the peak of his career, however, he weighed over 300 pounds. He was then known as the Jazz Jelly, but he went on a diet. He wasn't dieting when I was working for him. He ate anything and everything in sight. Watching him put away oysters was an education in itself!

WHITEMAN OYSTERS

3 dozen oysters on the half-shell
ice
lemon slices
Cocktail Sauce

On large platter, spread ice. Embed oysters on ice, garnish with lemon slices; put sauce at side or in middle.

COCKTAIL SAUCE

2 tbsp. horseradish
6 tbsp. catsup
1 tbsp. Worcestershire sauce
4 tbsp. lemon juice
celery salt
dash of Tabasco

Mix all ingredients and serve.

I met Al Jolson through my radio show, and to me, he is still Mr. Show Business. I think this man exerts a powerful influence on the comics and entertainers of today. He was the first performer to really relax on stage—you know, loosen his tie, take off his jacket, sit down on the apron (near the footlights), and just talk to his audiences. Jolson was in town to do publicity for *The Jolson Story* when he first appeared on my show. We got to be very good friends, and he came on again and again. He kept telling me he knew I'd end up in television and that when I did he'd be my first guest. Well, he was right, and I did get my own TV show, but by that time Jolson was dead. However, I put him on and on and on. How? Well, I'll explain. There's never a day passes that I don't find a way of mentioning his name. As long as my TV show lasts, he will always be my favorite guest, my mascot, my good-luck charm, with me in spirit if not on camera. Watch and listen, and you'll see what I mean. When I finish the program, I still think of him when I go over to Nathan's Famous. In the old days, when he was still around to call me "Sonny Boy," Jolson and I enjoyed Broadway's favorite: the hot pastrami sandwich.

HOT PASTRAMI SANDWICH

- 3 large (from center of loaf) slices of Jewish rye or corn bread
- mayonnaise
- ½ lb. cole slaw
- as much pastrami as you like
- ¼ cup Russian dressing
- 1 hard-boiled egg yolk (optional)
- mustard
- lettuce

Spread 1 slice of bread with mayonnaise. Add cole slaw and a few slices of pastrami. Top with mayonnaise. On top of the second slice, spread mayonnaise, mustard, and cole slaw, top with pastrami and top pastrami with Russian dressing and mashed egg yolk. Spread last piece of bread with mustard. Dill pickles are good as a side dish.

Eddie Cantor tells Rita Johnson a thing or two in *Forty Little Mothers.*

Ebullient Eddie, they called him, and Banjo Eyes. I'm talking about Eddie Cantor, the kid. You always thought of him as perennially young, or at least I did. He was another comedian who came up the hard way, and though he made it big in practically all branches of show business, he never forgot his early struggles. He didn't want his five daughters to forget them, either. He was afraid they'd start taking things for granted, and he always thought you should save for a rainy day. One time he was explaining to his daughters how he starved while he was knocking on managers' doors in little old cold New York. They listened solemnly to the recital of his vicissitudes, he told me, and when he had reached an impressive and even tearful finale, one of them topped him by saying solemnly, "Gee, Pop, aren't you glad you live with us, now?"

I had dinner with Eddie several times, and at his house I was served a borscht I shall never forget. I really remember it because that was one of the times I had the nerve to ask for the recipe. Here it is:

EDDIE CANTOR'S BORSCHT

6 cups beef broth (use bouillon cubes)
1 cup shredded beets
1 cup shredded carrots
1 cup minced onions
1½ cups shredded cabbage
½ green pepper, shredded
salt and pepper, to taste
½ cup canned tomatoes
½ cup sour cream

In a large saucepan put broth, beets, carrots, and

onions. Cook over low flame until tender. Add cabbage, green pepper, salt, and pepper (season generously). Cook 5 minutes more. Add tomatoes. Cook 5 minutes more. Serve with sour cream for each portion. (Serves 4–6)

Of my four best friends in show business—Whiteman, Jolson, Cantor, and Rudy Vallee—there are three I can't see anymore unless I look at their film clips. But Rudy Vallee is still around and

Crooner with a megaphone and a reputation for thrift: **Rudy Vallee**

spends a lot of his time in New York, too. Maybe this generation knows Rudy only by name, but my generation loved Vallee. His name was synonymous with hope in the despairing years of the Depression. Millions of downhearted people were uplifted by the sound of his cheerful voice toasting "Dear Old Maine," or telling you that there was a rainbow "just around the corner." He was the first of the great crooners and one of that era's three Yale immortals—along with Peter Arno, the cartoonist, and Albie Booth, the football star. Today, Rudy Vallee is much the same as he was in the years when he was lifting a megaphone to his lips and giving out with songs in many a motion picture. He is just as handsome and just as charming and, Depression notwithstanding, he is rich. He made it before taxes, and he kept it. Rudy believes in being thrifty with everything except his talent and his entertaining. The last time I was in Hollywood, visiting on his hilltop—yes, another hacienda—I had a couple of Spanish dishes that were really tops. And again, I had the nerve to ask for the recipes. Here they are:

CEVICHE

1 lb. fresh filet red snapper or striped bass
juice of 3 limes
juice of 3 lemons
1 garlic clove, finely chopped
1 Jalapeño pepper (fresh or canned), chopped
½ tsp. salt
⅛ tsp. white pepper
2 tbsp. finely chopped chives and parsley
1 sweet potato
1 cob corn
½ head lettuce
1 medium red onion, thinly sliced

Remove skin and bone of fish. Slice in 1/8- to 1/4-inch slices. Put fish in bowl. Mix juice of limes and lemons, garlic, Jalapeño pepper, salt, white pepper, chives, and parsley. Pour over fish. Cover bowl and refrigerate for 1 hour. Cook potato in skin. Cook corn the usual way. Cool. Cut corn and potato in 1-inch slices.

Serve on lettuce arranged on china (not silver) platter. After arranging fish on lettuce, circle with corn and slices of peeled sweet potato. Garnish with onion rings. (Serves 4–6)

BASS VALLEE

6 filets striped bass or red snapper, fresh or frozen
juice of 2 lemons
1 tsp. salt
1/8 tsp. paprika
dash of white pepper
1 cup light cream
2 whole eggs, beaten
2 tsp. salad oil
2 tbsp. flour
4 tbsp. vegetable shortening
4 tbsp. butter
10 cherry tomatoes
5 parsley potatoes (see page 148)

Place filets in shallow dish or pan. Mix lemon juice, salt, paprika, and pepper, and pour over fish, dividing evenly among 6 filets. Steep in marinade for 10 minutes. Add cream,

INDEX

Joe Franklin's business is nostalgia. His anecdotes and interviews with stars of the past have been entertaining movie fans for years. His nightly radio conversations with celebrities on the "Joe Franklin Show" are favorite listening for connoisseurs. Mr. Franklin is also host of two television programs, "When Movies Were Movies" and "Memory Lane."

Florence Stevenson is the author of five novels. Her articles also appear in *High Fidelity, Stereo Review, Opera News,* and other music publications.